Smith Wigglesworth

on Spiritual Gifts

Other Titles by Smith Wigglesworth

Smith Wigglesworth

on Spiritual Gifts

Smith
Wigglesworth

Whitaker House

Whitaker House gratefully acknowledges and thanks Glenn Gohr
and the entire staff of the Assemblies of God Archives in
Springfield, Missouri, for graciously assisting us in compiling
Smith Wigglesworth's works for publication
in this book.

Publisher's note:
This book has been edited for the modern reader. Words, expressions, and
sentence structure have been updated for clarity and readability. Although the
New King James Version quoted in this edition was not available to the author,
the Bible versions used were carefully and prayerfully selected in order to
make the language of the entire text readily understandable while maintaining
Wigglesworth's original premises and message.

Unless otherwise indicated, all Scripture quotations are taken from the *New
King James Version*, © 1979, 1980, 1982, 1984 by Thomas Nelson, Inc. Used
by permission. All rights reserved. Scripture quotations marked (KJV) are
taken from the King James Version of the Holy Bible.

SMITH WIGGLESWORTH ON SPIRITUAL GIFTS

ISBN-13: 978-0-88368-533-4
ISBN-10: 0-88368-533-7
Printed in the United States of America
© 1998 by Whitaker House

Whitaker House
1030 Hunt Valley Circle
New Kensington, PA 15068
www.whitakerhouse.com

Library of Congress Cataloging-in-Publication Data
Wigglesworth, Smith, 1859–1947.
Smith Wigglesworth on spiritual gifts / by Smith Wigglesworth.
p.   cm.
ISBN 0-88368-533-7 (trade paper: alk. paper)
1. Gifts, Spiritual. 2. Pentecostal churches—Doctrines. I. Title.
BT767.3.W5 1998
234'.13—dc21   98-21710

6 7 8 9 10 11 12 13 14 **W** 14 13 12 11 10 09 08 07

CONTENTS

INTRODUCTION

An encounter with Smith Wigglesworth was an unforgettable experience. This seems to be the universal reaction of all who knew him or heard him speak. Smith Wigglesworth was a simple yet remarkable man who was used in an extraordinary way by our extraordinary God. He had a contagious and inspiring faith. Under his ministry, thousands of people came to salvation, committed themselves to a deeper faith in Christ, received the baptism in the Holy Spirit, and were miraculously healed. The power that brought these kinds of results was the presence of the Holy Spirit, who filled Smith Wigglesworth and used him in bringing the good news of the Gospel to people all over the world. Wigglesworth gave glory to God for everything that was accomplished through his ministry, and he wanted people to understand his work only in this context, because his sole desire was that people would see Jesus and not himself.

Smith Wigglesworth was born in England in 1859. Immediately after his conversion as a boy, he had a concern for the salvation of others and won people to Christ, including his mother. Even so, as a young man, he could not express himself well enough to give a testimony in church, much less preach a sermon. Wigglesworth said that his mother had the same difficulty in expressing herself that he did. This family trait, coupled with the fact that he had no formal education because he began working twelve hours a day at the age of seven to help support the family, contributed to Wigglesworth's awkward speaking style. He became a plumber by trade, yet he continued to devote himself to winning many people to Christ on an individual basis.

In 1882, he married Polly Featherstone, a vivacious young woman who loved God and had a gift of preaching and evangelism. It was she who taught him to read and who became his closest confidant and strongest supporter. They both had compassion for the poor and needy in their community, and they opened a mission, at which Polly preached. Significantly, people were miraculously healed when Wigglesworth prayed for them.

In 1907, Wigglesworth's circumstances changed dramatically when, at the age of forty-eight, he was baptized in the Holy Spirit. Suddenly, he had a new power that enabled him to preach, and even his wife was amazed at the transformation. This was the beginning of what became a worldwide evangelistic and healing ministry that reached thousands. He eventually ministered in the United States, Australia, South Africa, and all over Europe. His ministry extended up to the time of his death in 1947.

Several emphases in Smith Wigglesworth's life and ministry characterize him: a genuine, deep compassion for the unsaved and sick; an unflinching belief in the Word of God; a desire that Christ should increase and he should decrease (John 3:30); a belief that he was called to exhort people to enlarge their faith and trust in God; an emphasis on the baptism in the Holy Spirit with the manifestation of the gifts of the Spirit as in the early church; and a belief in complete healing for everyone of all sickness.

Smith Wigglesworth was called "The Apostle of Faith" because absolute trust in God was a constant theme of both his life and his messages. In his meetings, he would quote passages from the Word of God and lead lively singing to help build people's faith and encourage them to act on it. He emphasized belief in the fact that God could do the impossible. He had great faith in what God could do, and God did great things through him.

Wigglesworth's unorthodox methods were often questioned. As a person, Wigglesworth was reportedly courteous, kind, and gentle. However, he became forceful when dealing with the Devil, whom he believed caused all sickness. Wigglesworth said the reason he spoke bluntly and acted forcefully with people was that he knew he needed to get their attention so they could focus on God. He also had such anger toward the Devil and sickness that he acted in a seemingly rough way. When he prayed for people to be healed, he would often hit or punch them at the place of their problem or illness. Yet, no one was hurt by this startling treatment. Instead, they were remarkably healed. When he was asked why he treated people in this manner, he said that he was not hitting the people but that he was hitting the Devil. He believed that Satan should never be treated gently or allowed to get away with anything. About twenty people were reportedly raised from the dead after he prayed for them. Wigglesworth himself was healed of appendicitis and kidney stones, after which his personality softened and he was more gentle with those who came to him for prayer for healing. His abrupt manner in ministering may be attributed to the fact that he was very serious about his calling and got down to business quickly.

Although Wigglesworth believed in complete healing, he encountered illnesses and deaths that were difficult to understand. These included the deaths of his wife and son, his daughter's lifelong deafness, and his own battles with kidney stones and sciatica.

He often seemed paradoxical: compassionate but forceful, gentle but blunt, a well-dressed gentleman whose speech was often ungrammatical or confusing. However, he loved God with everything he had, he was steadfastly committed to God and to His Word, and he didn't rest until he saw God move in the lives of those who needed Him.

In 1936, Smith Wigglesworth prophesied about what we now know as the charismatic movement. He accurately predicted that the established mainline denominations would experience revival and the gifts of the Spirit in a way that would surpass even the Pentecostal movement. Wigglesworth did not live to see the renewal, but as an evangelist and prophet with a remarkable healing ministry, he had a tremendous influence on both the Pentecostal and charismatic movements, and his example and influence on believers is felt to this day.

Without the power of God that was so obviously present in his life and ministry, we might not be reading transcripts of his sermons, for his spoken messages were often disjointed and ungrammatical. However, true gems of spiritual insight shine through them because of the revelation he received through the Holy Spirit. It was his life of complete devotion and belief in God and his reliance on the Holy Spirit that brought the life-changing power of God into his messages.

As you read this book, it is important to remember that Wigglesworth's works span a period of several decades, from the early 1900s to the 1940s. They were originally presented as spoken rather than written messages, and necessarily retain some of the flavor of a church service or prayer meeting. Some of the messages were Bible studies that Wigglesworth led at various conferences. At his meetings, he would often speak in tongues and give the interpretation, and these messages have been included as well. Because of Wigglesworth's unique style, the sermons and Bible studies in this book have been edited for clarity, and archaic expressions that would be unfamiliar to modern readers have been updated.

In conclusion, we hope that as you read these words of Smith Wigglesworth, you will truly sense his complete trust and unwavering faith in God and take to heart one of his favorite sayings: "Only believe!"

ONE

CONCERNING SPIRITUAL GIFTS

od wants us to enter into the rest of faith. He desires us to have all confidence in Him. He purposes that His Word will be established in our hearts; and, as we believe His Word, we will see that *"all things are possible"* (Matt. 19:26).

In 1 Corinthians 12:1 we read, *"Now concerning spiritual gifts, brethren, I do not want you to be ignorant."* There is a great weakness in the church of Christ because of an awful ignorance concerning the Spirit of God and the gifts He has come to bring. God wants us to be powerful in every way because of the revelation of the knowledge of His will concerning the power and manifestation of His Spirit. He desires us to be continually hungry to receive more and more of His Spirit.

In the past, I have organized many conferences, and I have found that it is better to have a man on my platform who has not received the baptism but who is hungry for all that God has for him, than a man who has received the baptism and is satisfied and has settled down and become stationary and stagnant. But of course I would prefer a man who is baptized with the Holy Spirit and is still hungry for more of God. A man who is not hungry to receive more of God is out of order in any Christian conference.

THE IMPORTANCE OF BEING FILLED

It is impossible to overestimate the importance of being filled with the Spirit. It is impossible for us to meet the conditions of the day, to *"walk in the light as He is in the light"* (1 John 1:7), to subdue kingdoms and work righteousness and bind the power of Satan, unless we are filled with the Holy Spirit.

We read that, in the early church, *"they continued steadfastly in the apostles' doctrine and fellowship, in the breaking of bread, and in prayers"* (Acts 2:42). It is important for us also to continue steadfastly in these same things.

For some years I was associated with the Plymouth Brethren. They are very strong on the Word and are sound on water baptism. They do not neglect the communion service; rather, they have it on the morning of every Lord's Day, as the early church did. These people seem to have the wood and the kindling, but not the match. If they had the fire, then they would be all ablaze.

Because they lack the fire of the Holy Spirit, there is no life in their meetings. One young man who attended their meetings received the baptism with the speaking in other tongues as the Spirit gave

14

utterance (Acts 2:4). The brethren were very upset about this, and they came to the young man's father and said to him, "You must take your son aside and tell him to cease." They did not want any disturbance. The father told the son, "My boy, I have been attending this church for twenty years and have never seen anything of this kind. We are established in the truth and do not want anything new. We won't have it." The son replied, "If that is God's plan, I will obey, but somehow or other I don't think it is." As they were going home, the horse stood still; the wheels of their carriage were in deep ruts. The father pulled at the reins, but the horse did not move. He asked, "What do you think is up?" The son answered, "It has gotten established." God save us from becoming stationary.

God wants us to understand spiritual gifts and to *"earnestly desire the best gifts"* (1 Cor. 12:31). He also wants us to enter into the *"more excellent way"* (v. 31) of the fruit of the Spirit. We must implore God for these gifts. It is a serious thing to have the baptism and yet be stationary. To live two days in succession on the same spiritual plane is a tragedy. We must be willing to deny ourselves everything to receive the revelation of God's truth and to receive the fullness of the Spirit. Only that will satisfy God, and nothing less must satisfy us.

A young Russian received the Holy Spirit and was mightily clothed with power from on high. The secret of his power was a continuous waiting upon God. As the Holy Spirit filled him, it seemed as though every breath became a prayer, and so his entire ministry was continually increasing.

15

I knew a man who was full of the Holy Spirit and would only preach when he knew that he was mightily anointed by the power of God. He was once asked to preach at a Methodist church. He was staying at the minister's house and he said, "You go on to church and I will follow." The place was packed with people, but this man did not show up. The Methodist minister, becoming anxious, sent his little girl to inquire why he did not come. As she came to the bedroom door, she heard him crying out three times, "I will not go." She went back and reported that she had heard the man say three times that he would not go. The minister was troubled about it, but almost immediately afterward the man came in. As he preached that night, the power of God was tremendously manifested. The preacher later asked him, "Why did you tell my daughter that you were not coming?" He answered, "I know when I am filled. I am an ordinary man, and I told the Lord that I did not dare to go and would not go until He gave me a fresh filling of the Spirit. The moment the glory filled me and overflowed, I came to the meeting."

Yes, there is a power, a blessing, an assurance, a rest in the presence of the Holy Spirit. You can feel His presence and know that He is with you. You do not need to spend an hour without this inner knowledge of His holy presence. With His power upon you, there can be no failure. You are above par all the time.

"You know that you were Gentiles, carried away to these dumb idols, however you were led" (1 Cor. 12:2). This is the age of the Gentiles. When the Jews refused the blessings of God, He scattered them, and

He has grafted the Gentiles into the olive tree where many of the Jews were broken off. (See Romans 11:17–25.) There has never been a time when God has been so favorable to a people who were not a people. (See 1 Peter 2:9–10.) He has brought in the Gentiles to carry out His purpose of preaching the Gospel to all nations and receiving the power of the Holy Spirit to accomplish this task. It is because of the mercy of God that He has turned to the Gentiles and made us partakers of all the blessings that belong to the Jews. Here, under this canopy of glory, because we believe, we get all the blessings of faithful Abraham.

GUARD AGAINST ERROR

Therefore I make known to you that no one speaking by the Spirit of God calls Jesus accursed, and no one can say that Jesus is Lord except by the Holy Spirit. (1 Cor. 12:3)

Many evil, deceiving spirits have been sent forth in these last days who endeavor to rob Jesus of His lordship and of His rightful place. Many people are opening the doors to these latest devils, such as New Theology and New Thought and Christian Science. These evil cults deny the fundamental truths of God's Word. They all deny eternal punishment and the deity of Jesus Christ. You will never see the baptism of the Holy Spirit come upon a man who accepts these errors. Nor will you see anyone receive the baptism who puts Mary in the place of the Holy Spirit. No one can know he is saved by works. If you ever speak to someone who believes this, you will know that he is not definite on the matter of the new birth. He cannot be. And there is another thing: you will never find a Jehovah's Witness baptized in the Holy Spirit. The same is true for a member of any other cult who does not believe that the Lord Jesus Christ is preeminent.

The all-important thing is to make Jesus Lord of your life. Men can become lopsided by emphasizing the truth of divine healing. Men can get into error by preaching on water baptism all the time. But we never go wrong in exalting the Lord Jesus Christ, in giving Him the preeminent place and glorifying Him as both Lord and Christ, yes, as "very God of very God." As we are filled with the Holy Spirit, our one desire is to glorify Him. We need to be filled with the Spirit to get the full revelation of the Lord Jesus Christ.

God's command is for us to *"be filled with the Spirit"* (Eph. 5:18). We are no good if we only have a full cup. We need to have an overflowing cup all the time. It is a tragedy not to live in the fullness of overflowing. See that you never live below the overflowing tide.

USE THE GIFTS PROPERLY

"There are diversities of gifts, but the same Spirit" (1 Cor. 12:4). Every manifestation of the Spirit is given *"for the profit of all"* (v. 7). When the Holy Spirit is moving in an assembly of believers and His gifts are in operation, everyone will profit.

I have seen some people who have been terribly off track. They believe in gifts—prophecy, in particular—and they use these gifts apart from the power of the Holy Spirit. We must look to the Holy Spirit to show us how to use the gifts, what they are for, and when to use them, so that we may never use them without the power of the Holy Spirit. I do not know of anything that is so awful today as people using a gift without the power. Never do it. God save us from doing it.

While a man who is filled with the Holy Spirit may not be conscious of having any gift of the Spirit, the gifts can be made manifest through him. I have gone to many places to minister, and I have found that, under the unction, or anointing, of the Holy Spirit, many wonderful things have happened in the midst of the assembly when the glory of the Lord was upon the people. Any man who is filled with God and filled with His Spirit might at any moment have any of the nine gifts listed in 1 Corinthians 12 made manifest through him, without knowing that he has a gift.

Sometimes I have wondered whether it is better to be always full of the Holy Spirit and to see signs and wonders and miracles without any consciousness of possessing a gift or whether it is better to know one has a gift. If you have received the gifts of the Spirit and they have been blessed, you should never under any circumstances use them without the power of God upon you pressing the gift through. Some have used the prophetic gift without the holy touch, and they have come into the realm of the natural. It has brought ruin, caused dissatisfaction, broken hearts, and upset assemblies. Do not seek the gifts unless you have purposed to abide in the Holy Spirit. They should be manifested only in the power of the Holy Spirit.

USE THE GIFTS WITH WISDOM

The Lord will allow you to be very drunk in the Spirit in His presence, but sober among people. I like to see people so filled with the Spirit that they are drunk in the Spirit like the 120 disciples were on the Day of Pentecost, but I don't like to see people drunk in the Spirit in the wrong place. That is what troubles us: somebody being drunk in the Spirit in a place of worship where a lot of people come in who know nothing about the Word. If you allow yourself to be drunk there, you send people away; they look at you instead of seeing God. They condemn the whole thing because you have not been sober at the right time.

Paul wrote, *"For if we are beside ourselves, it is for God; or if we are of sound mind, it is for you"* (2 Cor. 5:13). You can be beside yourself. You can go a bit further than being drunk; you can dance, if you will do it at the right time. So many things are commendable when all the people are in the Spirit. Many things are very foolish if the people around you are not in the Spirit. We must be careful not to have a good time in the Lord at the expense of somebody else. When you have a good time, you must see that the spiritual conditions in the place lend themselves to it and that the people are falling in line with you. Then you will always find it a blessing.

While it is right to earnestly desire the best gifts, you must recognize that the all-important thing is to be filled with the power of the Holy Spirit Himself. You will never have trouble with people who are filled with the power of the Holy Spirit, but you will have a lot of trouble with people who have the gifts but no power. The Lord does not want us to *"come short"* in any gift (1 Cor. 1:7). But at the same time, He wants us to be so filled with the Holy Spirit that it will be the Holy Spirit manifesting Himself through the gifts. Where the glory of God alone is desired, you can expect that every gift that is needed will be made manifest. To glorify God is better than to idolize gifts. We prefer the Spirit of God to any gift; but we can see the manifestation of the Trinity in the gifts: different gifts but the same Spirit, different administrations but the same Lord, diversities of operation but the same God working all in all (1 Cor. 12:4–6). Can you conceive of what it will mean for our triune God to be manifesting Himself in His fullness in our assemblies?

Imagine a large locomotive boiler that is being filled with steam. You can see the engine letting off some of the steam as it remains stationary. It looks as though the whole thing might burst. You can see believers who are like that. They start to scream, but that does not edify anyone. However, when the locomotive moves on, it serves the purpose for which it was built and pulls along many cars with goods in them. It is the same way with believers when they are operating in the gifts of the Spirit properly.

Inward Power Manifested Outwardly

It is wonderful to be filled with the power of the Holy Spirit and for Him to serve His own purposes through us. Through our lips, divine utterances flow, our hearts rejoice, and our tongues are glad. It is an inward power that is manifested in outward expression. Jesus Christ is glorified. As your faith in Him is

TWO

UNDERSTANDING THE GIFTS

et us review the twelfth chapter of 1 Corinthians. The first verse reads, *"Now concerning spiritual gifts, brethren, I do not want you to be ignorant."* When the Holy Spirit says that, He expects us to understand what the gifts are, and He wants us to understand that the church may be able to profit by them.

First, let us examine the nature of those who are led by the Spirit. *"No one can say that Jesus is Lord except by the Holy Spirit"* (1 Cor. 12:3). Whenever I have come in contact with people who have acknowledged the Lord Jesus, I have known whether they knew anything about the Spirit of God. For every spirit that is of God testifies of Jesus, and you will always be able to tell people's spiritual condition by that. If they do not confess that Jesus was manifested in the flesh, you may know that they do not have the Spirit of God (v. 3). Beloved, on the contrary, we find that every spirit that confesses that Jesus is Lord does so by the Holy Spirit.

GREAT POSSIBILITIES

Everyone who has received the Holy Spirit has within him great possibilities and unlimited power.

He also has great possessions, not only of things that are present but also of things that are to come (1 Cor. 3:22). The Holy Spirit has power to equip you for every emergency. The reason people are not thus equipped is that they do not receive Him and do not yield to Him. They are timid and they doubt, and in the measure that they doubt, they go down. But if you will yield to His leading and not doubt, it will lead you to success and victory. You will grow in grace, and you will have not only a controlling power but also a power that reveals the mind of God and the purposes He has for you. I see that all things are in the power of the Holy Spirit, and I must not fail to give you the same truth.

MANIFESTING THE GLORY OF GOD

We must remember that we have entered into the manifestation of the glory of God, and there is great power and strength in that. Many believers might be far ahead of where they are now spiritually, but they have doubted. If by any means the Enemy can come in and make you believe a lie, he will do so. We have had to struggle to maintain our standing in our salvation, for the Enemy would beat us out of it, if possible. It is in the closeness of the association and oneness with Christ that there is no fear, but perfect confidence all the time. The child of God does not need to go back a day for his experience, for the presence of the Lord is with him and the Holy Spirit is in him, in mighty power, if he will believe. I see that we should stir one another up and provoke one another to good works (Heb. 10:24).

The Pentecostal people have a "know" in their experience. We know that we have the Spirit abiding within, and if we are not moved upon by the Spirit, we move the Spirit; that is what we mean by "stirring up the Spirit." And yet it is not we but the living faith within us—it is the Spirit who stirs Himself up.

FAITH

We should ask ourselves, "Where are we living?" I do not mean in the natural. We are a spiritual people, *"a royal priesthood,"* a holy people (1 Pet. 2:9). If we find that there is unbelief in us, we must search our hearts to see why it is there. Where there is a living faith, there is no unbelief, and we go on from faith to faith until it becomes as natural to live there as can be. But if you try to live by faith before you have been justified in Christ, you will fail, for *"the just shall live by faith"* (Rom. 1:17). When you are justified, it is a natural consequence for you to live by faith. It is easy; it is joyful. It is more than that: it is our life and spiritual inheritance.

If the Spirit can stir you up, you will not *"come short"* (1 Cor. 1:7) in any gift. God wants you to see that we do not need to come short in any gift, and He wants to bring us to a place where we will be on fire because of what He has called us to. We should always move the tent every night; we cannot stay in one place. The land is before us; there are wonderful possessions to be had. God says, "They are yours; go in and claim them."

Paul prayed that we might *"be able to comprehend with all the saints"* (Eph. 3:18). I see the place where Paul was in the Holy Spirit, and I believe that God is calling us today to comprehend as much as Paul comprehended. It is in the perfect will of God that we should possess the needed gifts, but there must be unity between God and you. When the gifts are in evidence, the whole church is built up, Christ being the Head.

> *There are diversities of activities, but it is the same God who works all in all. But the manifestation of the Spirit is given to each one for the profit of all.* (1 Cor. 12:6–7)

THE POWER OF YIELDING TO GOD

Jesus said, *"Behold, I have come to do Your will, O God!"* (Heb. 10:9), and as we surrender in that way, God will be delighted to hand to us the gift that is necessary. The more we realize that God has furnished us with a gift, the more completely we will be united with Jesus, so that people will be conscious of Him rather than of His gift.

Oh, beloved, if everything is not of the Holy Spirit, and if we are not so lost and controlled in the ministry of the gift that it is only to be Jesus, it will all be a failure and come to nothing. There were none so self-conscious as those who said, *"In Your name, [we have] cast out demons"* (Matt. 7:22). They were so controlled by the natural and the thought that they had done it all, that God was not in it. But when He comes forth and does it, it is all right.

There is a place in the Holy Spirit where we will not allow unbelief to affect us, for God has all power in heaven and earth. And now that I am in the secret knowledge of this power, I stand in a place where my faith is not to be limited because I have the knowledge that He is in me and I in Him.

Some of you have come from your homes with broken hearts; you have a longing for something to strengthen you in the midst of the conditions that exist there, and a power to make these conditions different. You say you are *"unequally yoked together with unbelievers"* (2 Cor. 6:14). You have a mighty power that is greater than all natural power. You can take victory over your homes and your spouses and children, and you must do it in the Lord's way. Suppose you do see many things that ought to be different; if it is your cross, you must take it and win the victory for God. It can be done, for He who is in you is greater than all the power of hell (1 John 4:4). I believe that anyone filled with the Holy Spirit is equal to a legion of demons any day.

In a meeting in Glasgow, a man got up and said, "I have power to cast out demons." A man full of demons got up and came to him, and this man did everything he could, but he could not cast out the demons. Do you want to cast out demons? You be sure it is the Holy Spirit who does it. Recall that a slave girl who had a spirit of divination followed Paul around for many days (Acts 16:16–18) before he cast the demon out.

The Holy Spirit has His dwelling place within me and is stirring up my heart and life to adore Jesus. Other things must be left behind; I must adore Him.

WHAT IS YOUR MOTIVE?

God says, *"Everyone who asks receives"* (Matt. 7:8). What are you asking for? What is your motive? In the Scriptures we read, *"You ask and do not receive, because you ask amiss, that you may spend it on your pleasures"* (James 4:3). There is a need for the gifts, and God will reveal to you what you ought to have, and you should never be satisfied until you receive it.

It is important that we know we can do nothing in ourselves. However, we may know that we are clothed with the power of God so that, in a sense, we are not in the natural man. As we go forth in this power, things will take place as they took place in the days of the disciples.

When I received the new birth at eight years of age, it was so precious and lovely. Since that time, I have never lost the knowledge of my acceptance with God. Then, brothers and sisters, God did a wonderful work in me when I waited for the baptism.

I was in a strange position. For sixteen years I had testified to having received the baptism of the Holy Spirit, but I had really only received the anointing of the Spirit. In fact, I could not preach unless I had the anointing. My wife would come to me and say, "They are waiting for you to come out and speak to the people." I would say, "I cannot and will not come without the anointing of the Spirit."

I can see now that I was calling the anointing the baptism. But when the Holy Spirit came into my body until I could not give satisfaction to the glory that was in me, God took this tongue, and I spoke as the Spirit gave utterance, which brought perfect satisfaction to me. When He comes in, He abides. I then began to reach out as the Holy Spirit showed me.

ASK AND YOU WILL RECEIVE

In the call of the prophet Elisha, God saw the young man's willingness to obey. The twelve yoke of oxen, the plow, and all soon came to nothing; all bridges had to be burned behind him (1 Kings 19:19–21). Friend, the Lord has called you, too. Are you separated from the old things? You cannot go on unless you are.

As Elisha went on with the prophet Elijah, the young man heard wonderful things about Elijah's ministry, and he longed for the time when he would take his master's place. Now the time was getting close. His master said to him, "I am going to Gilgal today. I want you to remain here." "Master," he replied, "I must go with you." I see that other people also knew something about it, for they said to Elisha, "Do you know that your master is going to be taken away from you today?" He said, "Hold your peace; I know it." Later on, Elijah said, "I want to go on to Bethel. You stay here." But Elisha said, "No, I will not leave you." Something had been revealed to Elisha. Perhaps, in a similar way, God is drawing you to do something; you feel it.

Then Elijah said, "The Lord has sent me to Jordan. You stay here." It was the spirit of the old man that was stirring up the young man. If you see zeal in somebody else, reach out for it; it is for you. I am coming to realize that God wants all the members of His body joined together. In these days He is making us feel that when a person is failing to go on with God, we must restore that member.

When they came to the Jordan, Elijah struck his cloak on it and they crossed. No doubt Elisha said, "I must follow his steps." And when they had gone over, the old man said, "You have done well; you would not stay back. What is the real desire of your heart? I feel I am going to leave you. Ask what you like now, before I leave you." "Master," he said, "I have seen all that you have done. Master, I want twice as much as you have."

I believe it is the fainthearted who do not get much. As they went on up the hill, down came the chariot of fire, nearer and nearer, and when it landed, the old man jumped in and the young man said, "Father, Father, Father," and down came the cloak.

What have you asked for? Are you satisfied to continue on in the old way now that the Holy Spirit has come to give you an unlimited supply of power and says, "What will you have?" Why, we see that Peter was so filled with the Holy Spirit that his shadow falling on sick people healed them (Acts 5:15).

What do you want? Elisha asked, and he got it. He came down and said, "I don't feel any differently." However, he had the knowledge that feelings are not to be counted as anything; some of you are looking at your feelings all the time. He came to the waters of the Jordan as an ordinary man. Then, in the knowledge in which he possessed the cloak (not in any feelings about it), he said, "Where is the God of Elijah?" and he struck the water with the cloak. The waters parted and Elisha put his feet down in the river and crossed to the other side. When you put your feet down and say you are going to have a double portion, you will get it. After he had crossed, there were the young men again (they always come where there is power), and they said, "The spirit of Elijah rests on Elisha." (See 2 Kings 2:1–15.)

You are to have the gifts and to claim them. The Lord will certainly change your lives, and you will be new men and women. Are you asking for a double portion? I trust that no one will *"come short"* in any gift (1 Cor. 1:7). You say, "I have asked. Do you think God will be pleased if I ask again?" Yes, do so before Him. Ask again, and we may go forth in the Spirit of the cloak. Then we will no longer be working in our own strength but in the Holy Spirit's strength, and we will see and know His power because we believe.

THREE

GOD'S TREASURE HOUSE

ow inexhaustible is the treasure house of the Most High! How near God is to us when we are willing to draw near to Him! And how He comes and refreshes us when our hearts are attuned to Him and desire Him alone, for *"the desire of the righteous will be granted"* (Prov. 10:24).

God has for us today a divine experience that quickens, a divine life flowing through our beings that will be sufficient for us in all times of need. When God is for you, who can be against you (Rom. 8:31)? What a blessed assurance this is to the hungry heart. How it thrills one to the very depths of one's soul!

My heart's desire is to bring you again to a banquet, that wonderful spiritual reserve, that great blessed day of appointment for us with the King, so that you may believe that all the precious promises are *"Yes"* and *"Amen"* (2 Cor. 1:20) to us as we dare to believe.

Oh, to believe God! Oh, to rest upon what He says, for there is not one *"jot"* or *"tittle"* of the Word that will fail until all is fulfilled (Matt. 5:18)! Has He not promised, and will He not also perform (Rom. 4:21)? Our blessed Lord of life and glory impressed upon us before He left that He would send the Holy Spirit, the Comforter, and that, when the Spirit came, He would take of the words of Jesus and declare them to us (John 16:14–15). The Holy Spirit would pray through us, and whatever we would ask, the Lord would hear us (1 John 5:14–15).

So I want you to get in a definite place, daring to ask God for something that will be the means of stimulating your life forever.

Are you ready? You say, "What for?" To have some of the promises fulfilled.

Are you ready? What for? For God to so clothe you with the Spirit this day that there will be nothing within you that will war against the Spirit. Are you ready? Search your heart diligently.

Are you ready? What for? For you to know the Word of God. For you to know that they who dwell and live in the Spirit of God are kept in a perfect state in which there is no condemnation. (See Romans 8:1.)

I want very much for you to get stirred up with the prospect of this state and then to come into the experience of this state, because that is what God wants you to have. He wants you to get so moved by the power of God that you believe that the things you are hearing about will be yours.

So many people miss a great many things because they are always thinking that they are for someone else. I want you to know that God's Word is for you and that you are to make a personal application of all there is in the Scriptures.

I do not believe that the Scriptures are only for pastors, teachers, evangelists, prophets, or apostles. They are for the whole body of Christ, for it is the body that has to be the epistle of Christ. So the Word of God has to abound in you until you are absolutely built and fixed upon the living Word.

ALL GIFTS ARE FOR EDIFICATION

I am going to remind you of 1 Corinthians 14:12, because I want to make it the keynote of everything I am presenting to you here on the topic of spiritual gifts:

> *Even so you, since you are zealous for spiritual gifts, let it be for the edification of the church that you seek to excel.*

Keep that definitely in mind because, whatever gifts are manifested in a service, they mean nothing to me unless they edify or comfort or console.

God wants to make you worthy of His wonderful name. You must always understand that all the gifts and graces of the Spirit are most helpful to you when you are a blessing to others. The Holy Spirit did not come to exalt you; He came so that you could exalt the Lord.

Before these services are over, I will be able to tell you definitely how to receive a gift and then how to use a gift or how to be in a place where the gift can be used. We should cover much ground because the Spirit is going to speak. If I were to use my own reasoning, you wouldn't be edified. There is only one edification that is going to last, and it is the spiritual, inward revelation of Christ. What is in the mind is no good unless it is spiritually quickened through the heart affections. So let us remember that it is more important that we are filled with the Holy Spirit, that the Spirit has His perfect control and way, than that we be filled with knowledge to no profit. *"Knowledge puffs up"* (1 Cor. 8:1). As the saying goes, "A little knowledge is dangerous." In fact, all knowledge is very dangerous unless it is balanced in a perfect place where God has the controlling position.

In the first few verses of 1 Corinthians 12, we find that the Holy Spirit is speaking through the apostle Paul. Paul's initial comment is that he does not want you to be ignorant concerning spiritual gifts. You are not to be ignorant of the best gift God has arranged for you. You are to come into possession. It is a will that has been left by God's Son. He rose to carry it out, and He is on the throne to carry out His own will. His will is that you should be filled with all the fullness of God. What a wonderful will!

The next thought is that, because we are Gentiles, God has entrusted to us the proclamation of the Gospel in the power and demonstration of the Spirit, so that we may not speak with man's wisdom but by the revelation of the operation of God.

So the Holy Spirit is to make us ready for every perfect work, ready in such a way that opportunities are taken advantage of. Just as much as if the Lord Jesus were in the world, we must be in the world, ready for the glorious, blessed anointing and equipping for service. In this way, the powers of hell will not prevail (Matt. 16:18); we will bind the powers of Satan. We will be in a great position to engage in spiritual battle.

INTERPRETATION OF TONGUES

The Spirit Himself brings forth light and truth to edify and build up the church in the most holy faith, that we might be ready for all activity in God. For the Spirit of the Lord is upon us to bring forth what God has declared and ordained, that we should go forth bearing precious fruit and come forth rejoicing, singing, and harvesting together.

Oh, to keep in the covenant place where you are hidden in Christ, where He alone is superseding, controlling, leading, directing, and causing you to live only for the glory of God!

THE UNCHANGEABLE WORD OF GOD

Let us move on to 1 Corinthians 12:3: *"No one speaking by the Spirit of God calls Jesus accursed."* Don't forget that you are entrusted with the Word of Life, which speaks to you as the Truth. Jesus was the Way, the Truth, and the Life (John 14:6), and He declared eternal life by the operation of the Gospel. For we receive immortality and life by the Gospel. Seeing these things are so, you can understand that those who receive the life of Christ move out of condemnation into eternal life.

But what about those who do not? They are still under condemnation, *"having no hope and without God in the world"* (Eph. 2:12) and in danger of eternal destruction. God save them!

Don't get away from the fact that Jesus is the personality of eternal death and eternal life. Hellfire will never be changed by what men say about it.

Hellfire will be the same forever. You will never change the Word of God by men's opinions. The Word of God is fixed forever (Isa. 40:8).

The Lord wants you to be in a significant place in which the Holy Spirit has such control of your inner eyes that He may reveal the fullness of the Lord of life until Jesus is glorified tremendously by the revelation of the Holy Spirit, until He becomes Lord over all things: your affections, your will, your purposes, your plans, and your wishes forever. Let Him be Lord.

INTERPRETATION OF TONGUES

For when the Lord changes the situation, then you come out of the hiding of captivity into the fullness of the revelation of the blaze of His glory, for when He has molded you, then He can build you and change you until He is having His way.

BUILDING YOUR CROWN OF GLORY

God has a great purpose for us in that we can be changed, and you are in a great place when you are willing to have this change take place. You are in a greater place when you are willing to drop everything that has brought you to where you thought you could not be changed; and when you have dropped all things that have hindered you, you have leaped forth and been tremendously changed.

If you have held anything from a human standpoint, no matter how it has come, that is not according to the biblical standard of the Word of God, let it be weeded out. If you do not get it weeded out, be warned: there is a time coming in which wood, hay, and stubble will be burned, but the gold, the silver, and the precious stones will stand the fire (1 Cor. 3:12–13).

Lots of people would like to know what kind of crown they will have when they get to glory. Well, the Lord will take everything that could not be burned by the fire and make your personal crown. So everybody is forming his own crown. Be careful not to be all wood, hay, and stubble. Have something left for the crown. There is a *"crown of glory that does not fade away"* (1 Pet. 5:4), which I am trying to help you build today.

A GIFT SPECIFICALLY FOR YOU

God has a special way of meeting the needs of individual people today. We all vary so much in our appearances, in how we are made. Yet God has a way of particularizing a gift so that it fits you perfectly, so that you will not be lopsided. I am trusting the Lord to help me to build you up so that you are not lopsided.

Lots of people have good things—but. Lots of people might be very remarkably used—but. Lots of people might soar into wonderful places of divine positions with God—but. And it is the "but" that spoils it.

Some people have very good gifts—all the gifts of God are good—but because the gifts have been made a blessing, these people transgress with the same gift and speak in tongues longer than they ought to. So it is the "but" that is in the way and that is spoiling the best.

Some people have prophecy, very wonderful prophecy, but there is a "but." They have prophesied, and the Lord has been with them in the prophecy, but because the people have applauded them, they have gone beyond divine prophecy and used their own human minds. The "but" has spoiled them until they do not want the hidden prophecy.

Mrs. So-and-So has a wonderful testimony, and we all like to hear her for three minutes, but we are all sick of it if she goes on for five minutes. Why is this so? There is a "but" about it.

Brother So-and-So ignites fire in every prayer meeting when he begins to speak, but after about five minutes, all the people say, "I wish he would stop." There is a "but" there.

It is because of the lopsidedness of people that I want to advise you so that you do not transgress. Do not use divine liberty to spoil God's position; rather, be wise, and the Lord will cause you to understand what it means. Be wise.

When you say that you have been baptized with the Holy Spirit, people look and say, "Well, if that is so, there ought to be something very beautiful about you."

Yes, it is true, and if there is something that is shady, something that is uncanny, something that does not express the glory or grace, the meekness or love of Christ, there is a "but" about it. The "but" is that you have not really gotten your own human spirit under control by the divine Spirit; the human is mingled with it, and it is spoiling the divine.

Now, a word to the wise is sufficient, and if you are not wise after you have heard it, it shows that you are foolish. Do not be foolish; be wise!

"Do not let your good be spoken of as evil" (Rom. 14:16). God wants people in these days who are so fortified, so built in Christ, that they do not need to be ashamed.

INTERPRETATION OF TONGUES

For it is God who has called you for His own purpose. It is Christ who ordained you, and being ordained by Christ we go forth to bring forth much fruit. God is being glorified when our anointing or our covenant with Christ is being reserved for God only, and we live and move for the glory of the exhibition of Christ. Then that is the place where Jesus is highly honored, and when you pray, God is glorified in the Son, and when you preach, the unction abides, and the Lord brings forth blessing upon the hearers.

DIVERSITIES OF GIFTS

In 1 Corinthians 12:4–7, you notice very re-markable words. In these verses we are dealing with the Spirit, with the Lord, and with God—each One of them in cooperation with this position:

There are diversities of gifts, but the same Spirit. There are differences of ministries, but the same Lord. And there are diversities of ac-tivities, but it is the same God who works all in all. But the manifestation of the Spirit is given to each one for the profit of all.

(1 Cor. 12:4–7)

There are diversities, varieties of gifts that truly are to be in the believer. There are nine gifts listed in 1 Corinthians 12, and I would like you to notice that they never interfere with the gifts that Jesus gave. If you will turn to Ephesians 4, you will find that Jesus gave gifts:

But to each one of us grace was given according to the measure of Christ's gift. Therefore He says: "When He ascended on high, He led captivity captive, and gave gifts to men."
(vv. 7–8)

A little later in the chapter, these gifts are listed:

And He Himself gave some to be apostles, some prophets, some evangelists, and some pastors and teachers, for the equipping of the saints for the work of ministry, for the edifying of the body of Christ. (vv. 11–12)

Let us look at the gifts Jesus has. How beautifully He arranges things. *"When He ascended on high, He led captivity captive, and gave gifts to men"* (Eph. 4:8).

Now, the apostle Paul was in captivity. How do we know? He described his position as the chief of sinners (1 Tim. 1:15). By the way, as long as we know that the chief of sinners has been saved, every man that ever lives can be saved. Paul was the chief of sinners, and he was led captive when he was enraged with indignation against the disciples; he was rushing everywhere to apprehend them and put them in

40

prison and make them blaspheme (Acts 8:3; 9:1–2; 26:9–11).

So Paul was in captivity. Yet Jesus took him out of captivity; then He took him into His captivity and gave him gifts.

Jesus has already made disciples; He has gone up on high leading captivity captive; now He is giving gifts. This is the divine position of our Lord, giving gifts to those He has in captivity.

Now, who do you think is most likely to be in captivity? It is the people who are lost in God, who are hidden in Him.

Baptizing in water is an emblem of death, and the moment a person is immersed in the water, he is lifted out. But this is not the case with the baptism in the Holy Spirit. To be baptized in the Holy Spirit is to be in deeper every day, never lifted out, never coming out; it is to be in captivity, ready for gifts.

Now, is a person made a prophet or an apostle or a teacher before the baptism of the Spirit or after? I want to speak to you very definitely, and I want you to keep in mind what the Spirit will say to us at this time.

When I went to New Zealand, the power of God was very present, and God wonderfully worked miracles and wonders there. The gifts that laid hold of the whole place were the gifts of tongues and interpretation. That entire city was moved until the place that held 3,500 was often overcrowded, and we had 2,000 and 3,000 people who could not get in.

Now when the Plymouth Brethren, who knew the Word of God, saw the grace of God upon me, they wanted to have some conversation with me. So I gave them an audience, and eighteen of them came.

As soon as they began they said, "Well, we know God is with you; it is evident."

(In ten days we had 2,000 people saved, and we had 1,500 of those young converts sit down to communion; and it was the Plymouth Brethren who served us the wine and the bread.)

"Now," they said, "we want to examine the truth with you to see where things stand."

I said, "All right, brethren."

In a moment or two, they were quoting Ephesians to me.

"But, beloved," I said, "you know better than anybody that the man who climbs up some other way is a thief and a robber, don't you? How many times have you preached that? Jesus is the Door, and everyone entering that way will be saved. What does it mean? Jesus is Truth."

They continued quoting Ephesians to me.

"But, brethren," I said, "you have no right to Ephesians; you have no right to the epistles. The epistles are not for you. You are climbing up some other way."

Without fear of contradiction, on the authority of God, I say today that there is no person who has a right to the epistles until he has gone through the Acts of the Apostles and received the Holy Spirit.

They said I could not prove it. I said, "I can prove it very easily." And I read, *"For he who speaks in a tongue does not speak to men but to God, for no one understands him; however, in the spirit he speaks mysteries"* (1 Cor. 14:2).

"Now, brethren," I said, "tell me if you understand that."

They said, "No."

"That is simply because you have never received the Holy Spirit. Every person who receives the Holy Spirit receives that—speaking unto God by the Spirit. The Gospels are the Gospel of the kingdom of God. It is in the Acts of the Apostles that people see water baptism, sanctification, and also the receiving of the Holy Spirit fulfilled. So the moment you pass through the Acts of the Apostles, you are ready for the epistles, for the epistles were written to baptized believers.

"I will prove it another way," I continued, and I read Romans 8:26–27:

> *Likewise the Spirit also helps in our weaknesses. For we do not know what we should pray for as we ought, but the Spirit Himself makes intercession for us with groanings which cannot be uttered. Now He who searches the hearts knows what the mind of the Spirit is, because He makes intercession for the saints according to the will of God.*

Here is another distinct condition of a man filled with the Holy Spirit.

INTERPRETATION OF TONGUES
For the Lord Himself is the chief director of all truth, for He is the Way and the Truth; therefore, the Spirit takes the Word, which is Christ, and reveals it unto us, for He is the life by the Word. "He that heareth my word, and believeth on him that sent me, hath everlasting life." Jesus is the Way, Jesus is the Truth, Jesus is the Life.

The Holy Spirit is jealous over you. The Holy Spirit has a godly jealousy over you. Why? Lest you turn to yourself. He wants you to exhibit the Lord entirely. Therefore, He girds you. He sees to you in every way so that you will not be drawn aside by human desires but that, instead, Jesus will become the Alpha and Omega in all your desires.

Now, to this end the Spirit knows the great hunger of the heart. Hunger for what? For gifts, graces, beatitudes.

Oh, it is lovely when we are at a point at which we can only pray in the Holy Spirit!

Praying in the Spirit

I am going to give you a very important word about the usefulness of praying in the Spirit. Lots of people are still without an understanding of what it is to pray in the Spirit. In 1 Corinthians 14:15 we read, *"I will pray with the spirit, and I will also pray with the understanding. I will sing with the spirit, and I will also sing with the understanding."*

I am going to tell you a story that will help you to see how necessary it is that you be so lost in the order of the Holy Spirit that you will pray in the Holy Spirit.

Our missionary work in the center of Africa was opened by Brothers Burton and Salter, the latter being my daughter's husband. He is now there in the Congo. When they went there, there were four of them: Brothers Burton and Salter, an old man who wanted to go to help them build, and a young man who believed he was called to go. The old man died on the road and the young man turned back, so there were only two left.

They worked and labored. God was with them in a wonderful way. But Burton took sick, and all hopes were gone. Fevers are dreadful there; mosquitoes swarm; great evils are there. There he was, laid out; there was no hope. They covered him over and went outside very sorrowfully, because he truly was a pioneer missionary. They were in great distress and uttered words like this: "He has preached his last sermon."

When they were in that state, without any prompting whatever, Brother Burton stood right in the midst of them. He had arisen from his bed and had walked outside, and he now stood in the midst of them. They were astonished and asked how and what had happened.

All he could say was that he had been awakened out of a deep sleep with a warm thrill that went over his head, right down his body, and out through his toes.

"I feel so well," he said. "I don't know anything about my sickness."

It remained a mystery. Later, when he was over in England visiting, a lady said to him, "Brother Burton, do you keep a diary?"

"Yes," he said.

"Don't open the diary," she said, "until I talk with you."

"All right."

This is the story she told.

"At a certain time on a certain day, the Spirit of the Lord moved upon me. I was so moved by the power of the Spirit that I went alone into a place to pray. As I went there, believing that, just as usual, I was going to open my mouth and pray, the Spirit

45

laid hold of me and I was praying in the Spirit—not with understanding, but praying in the Spirit.

"As I prayed, I saw right into Africa; I saw you laid out helpless and, to all appearances, apparently dead. I prayed on until the Spirit lifted me, I knew I was in victory, and I saw you had risen up from that bed.

"Look at your diary, will you?"

He looked in the diary and found that it was exactly the same day.

So there are revivals to come; there are wonderful things to be done, when we can be lost in the Spirit until the Spirit prays through to victory.

INTERPRETATION OF TONGUES

It is only He; it is He who rolls away the cloud. He alone is the One who lifts the fallen, cheers the faint, brings fresh oil, and changes the countenance. It is the Lord your God. He has seen your misery, He has known your brokenheartedness, and He has known how near you seem to be to despair.

Oh, beloved, God is in the midst of us to help us into these wonderful divine places of appointment!

Are you ready? You say, "What for?" To let all differences cease and to have the same evidence the disciples had in the Upper Room.

Are you ready? What for? To be so in the place in which God's Son will be pleased that He gives you all the desires of your heart.

Are you ready? What for? So that God can fill you with new life, stimulate you with new fire. He can inflame you with great desire. We are in the midst of blessing; I want you to be blessed.

Faith has the greatest ability to position us. Faith is what will lift you into every place, if you do not interfere with it.

Don't forget you are in the presence of God. This day has to be covered with a greater day. It is not what you are; it is what you are intending to be.

If you have ever spoken in tongues, believe it is your right and your privilege to have anything in the Bible. Don't let your human mind interfere with the great plan of God. Submit yourself to God.

May the divine likeness of Him who is the express image of the Father dwell in you richly, abounding through all, supplying every need, bringing you into a place where you know the hand of God is leading you from treasure to treasure, from grace to grace, from victory to victory, from glory to glory, by the Spirit of the Lord.

FOUR

THE FRUIT AND THE GIFTS

s a preparation for the study of the gifts of the Spirit, we should read the twelfth chapter of Romans. All that is done and said in these meetings is upon the authority of the Word of God. I am sure it would not please God if we were to turn aside to any human thing when we have such a valuable, wonderful display of wisdom and authority in this living Word.

PARTAKERS OF THE DIVINE NATURE

We thank You, Lord, that You have made sufficient atonement for sin, sickness, deficiencies, all our weakness, and everything.

As we take our minds off human things and are clothed with the Spirit, we will be natural but also supernatural. This is a lovely condition. We are still natural, with just the same physique, just the same expression. We are the same people, only we are supernatural, inwardly displaying the revelation of the power of God through the same body. What a divine state!

Don't be afraid to understand that God intends for you to be *"partakers of the divine nature"* (2 Pet. 1:4), of divine life in the human frame, of divine thoughts over the human mind. You are to have your human minds transformed. The divine mind is to take its place so that you will always be the children of the Lord and act like people who are *"from above"* (John 3:31). You are *"from above"*; you are born of a *"new creation"* (2 Cor. 5:17). You were planted with Him (Rom. 6:5 KJV); you were risen, and you are to be seated with Him in the place of victory over the power of the Enemy.

Don't forget that God is in all, over all, through all. He is in you so that He might bring about in your daily ministries a divine plan as active and as perfect as the apostles had at the beginning, as Jesus had in His ministry. Jesus portrayed, showed forth, emphasized to His disciples this word: *"Be ye therefore perfect, even as your Father which is in heaven is perfect"* (Matt. 5:48 KJV).

We do not need to regard people according to the flesh anymore (2 Cor. 5:16). From this day, let us learn that we only need to know the character of the people according to the Spirit. Remember that the disciples came to a perfect place when they said, "We won't know Jesus anymore after the flesh." (See verse 16.)

They wouldn't remember Him in terms of His fleshly ministry. I don't mean a fleshly power, but His fleshly body. There were any number of things to remember about Jesus in terms of His natural human need, such as when He needed food from the tree and when He sat by the well and asked for water. We won't know Him that way anymore; we will know Jesus according to the Spirit.

What is the difference? He no longer has any human weakness but has perfect power over all weaknesses. May the Lord grant to us in these days a divine familiarity with the Master so that we begin from this day to be more and more spiritual until we live in the Spirit, not fulfilling the lusts of the flesh (Gal. 5:16), but living in Christ.

INTERPRETATION OF TONGUES

The Lord Himself feed us with the finest of the wheat. He seeks only to bring us into favor with the Father. He says, "Until now you have asked nothing"; ask large things, for my Father and I are one. And as you ask, it will be given you, a measure full, "pressed down, shaken together, and running over," that there will be no leanness in you, but you will be full, overflowing, expressive, God manifest in you, the glory of the Lord upon you, and He bringing forth songs in the earth.

FRUITS AND GIFTS UNITED

I want to speak a little about the dovetailing, the uniting together of the fruits and the gifts of the Spirit. I am just going to enumerate them so that you will know their relationship. This will be very profitable to you because you must be careful that whatever gift is manifested in you, it has to coincide, have a joint fellowship, with its corresponding fruit, so that you will never miss the plan of God in this holy order. Any gift that God may give you will never go to waste; it will always profit others.

The fruit of the Spirit is listed in Galatians 5:22–23: *"But the fruit of the Spirit is love, joy, peace, longsuffering, kindness, goodness, faithfulness, gentleness, self-control."* Now, let us see how the fruit corresponds to the gifts of the Spirit.

The first gift of the Spirit Paul mentioned in 1 Corinthians 12 is *"wisdom"* (v. 8), which must always be connected with love. Love is the first fruit; wisdom is the first gift.

The next gift is *"knowledge"* (v. 8). You will find, if you work this out, that knowledge will always bring joy and will be accompanied by joy. Knowledge produces joy, and they coincide.

The third is *"faith"* (v. 9). You never find that faith is to any profit unless there is peace, so the gift of faith coincides with the fruit of peace.

The next is *"healings"* (v. 9). You always find that the person who is used in healing is longsuffering. If he loses that, if the person who ministers to the needy does not enter into their need, well, remember the words in Philippians: *"The fellowship of His sufferings"* (Phil. 3:10). It doesn't mean that you have to go to the cross, but you have to be so in spirit with the needy sufferer that you enter right into his need.

In this regard, remember that you must be brought into a place of justification, because it may be that many of you are judging me and saying, "Isn't he rough when he ministers to people in healing!" Now, we must understand every man in his own way. You can't fill my boat, and I couldn't fill yours; but we can fill the boat God has made for us. We cannot turn aside to please humanity, because we have one Master, who is Christ.

A woman came before me in Australia where thousands were looking on, and I ministered to her for healing. She was a very large woman. As she came to me, the Spirit of the Lord revealed to me that inwardly there was an adversary destroying her life. Instantly, God helped me to rise up against the adversary, not against the woman.

In the name of Jesus, I dealt with this evil thing that had distressed the woman. With the whole crowd looking on, she cried, "You're killing me! You're killing me! Oh, you're killing me!"

She fell down on the floor. "Bring her back again," I said. I knew I had not finished the work.

Then I went at it again, destroying the evil that was there, and I knew I had to do it. The people did not understand as again she cried, "Oh, you're killing me!"

"Bring her back again," I said.

I laid my hands on her again in the name of Jesus, and the work was done. She walked five yards in the aisle, and the big cancer dropped off her.

You who are judging me, please leave your judgment outside, for I obey God. If you are afraid to be touched, don't come to me to pray for you. If you are not prepared to be dealt with as God leads me to deal, keep away. But if you can believe that God has me for a purpose, come, and I will help you.

How we need to have the mind of Christ and to live for Christ. What a serious thing it would be for me at sixty-eight years of age to try to please people when I have my Father in heaven to please!

INTERPRETATION OF TONGUES

It is the way into the treasure house the Lord brings you. It is not your way of thinking; it is the way in which He brings you through. Don't forget that Jesus said, "Straight is the gate, narrow the way" that brought you in to the plan and place of redemption with fullness. Therefore, do not resist the Spirit, do not judge the things, even prophecy, but lay hold of it that God is in the midst of you to bring you to the place of your desired health.

1 CORINTHIANS 13: A BALANCER

I now want to discuss the thirteenth chapter of 1 Corinthians. This chapter on love falls appropriately between the twelfth and the fourteenth chapters; it dovetails or unites the three chapters, bringing us into a place where we can understand them. The twelfth chapter deals with the gifts of the Spirit, the fourteenth chapter deals with the ministry of the gifts, and the thirteenth chapter deals with balance.

If you know anything about an engine, you know that right over the main throttle valve that lets the steam into the cylinder, with the piston driving it backward and forward, there are two little governor balls running around. Sometimes they go fast; sometimes they go slowly. They control the condition of the pistons so that the engine doesn't run away and so that it maintains an even motion.

That is exactly the purpose of the thirteenth chapter of 1 Corinthians; it shows believers how to keep the gifts in perfect harmony until we learn not to run away with them, not to get out of order. It shows that *"the wisdom that is from above"* (James 3:17) lies in a human vessel; it never loses its luster or glory or expression or force of character of divine origin.

So God has a plan for us. He wants to show us that even though our lives may be wonderful—for example, we may have the gift of divine prophecy, which is beautiful, or we may have all faith to move mountains (1 Cor. 13:2)—if we do not understand the Scriptures, if we lose the main factor, which will produce the governing principles, we become nothing. But if we are balanced by the power of the Spirit, every act will be an act of such divine quality that people will recognize that fact in a moment; their judgment will be accurate, as it was that day when the people saw Peter and John. (See Acts 3:1–4:4.) Although these disciples were humble men and had not gone through college courses, they had something that expressed a fact to the people: they had been in a place that had changed their character and their language; they had been with the Master (Acts 4:13).

While I know that many good things come out of colleges, you must not forget that you must occasionally go to night school, as Nicodemus did, and see the Master. (See John 3:1–21.)

A personal acquaintance with the Lord Jesus, by the revelation of the Spirit, can so move you that in an instant, you may have revelation that causes you to see that you are now encased by an enthronement of wisdom from on high.

INTERPRETATION OF TONGUES

"The wisdom which is from above is first peaceable, easily entreated, without partiality, full of goodness and truth," and the Lord of Hosts has us in His great pavilion of opening the avenue of our human nature, flowing forth through the natural life, divine life, quickened from on high, because we are the children of the King.

Thank you, Lord. We are the children of the King. We belong to the Lord; therefore, no other power has a right to us. We belong to Him.

INTERPRETATION OF TONGUES

From your mother's womb I called you. Though I have chastened you and put you through the fire, yet it was necessary to bring out of you and to bring you out into a land of promise. It is true that you have passed through deep waters and that the fire has many times seared you, but this was all to chasten you and to prove you, to see if you loved the Lord with all your heart. And now the Lord has brought you to the banquet. Eat, my beloved; eat, and be satisfied.

FIVE

HOW TO RECEIVE
A SPIRITUAL GIFT

The gift of the Holy Spirit, which He breathes into you, will make you wonderfully alive. It will almost seem as though you had never been born before. The jealousy God has over us, the interest He has in us, the purpose He has for us, the grandeur of His glory are so marvelous. God has called us into this place to receive gifts.

Now I want to tell you how to receive a gift. I will illustrate this by explaining the nature of a gift and telling you what happened to me when I received the gift of tongues.

The difference between speaking in tongues as a gift and speaking in tongues by receiving the Spirit is this: everybody who is baptized speaks as the Spirit gives utterance. The tongues that are manifested when someone receives the baptism are an evidence of the baptism. However, this is not the gift of tongues. The gift is a special manifestation in a person's life that he knows, and he can speak in

57

tongues as long as he wants to. Nevertheless, a person should never speak longer than the Spirit gives the anointing; he should never go beyond the Spirit's leading. Like someone giving a prophecy, he should never go beyond the spiritual anointing.

The trouble is this: after we have been blessed with tongues, our human nature often steps in. Everything that is not the rising tide of the Spirit is either law or letter. (See Romans 7:6–7.) What does this mean? When you are following the law, it means that you have fallen into your human nature. When you are following the letter, it means that you are depending upon the Word without the power. These two things will work against you instead of working for you.

The letter and the law bring harshness; the Spirit brings joy and happiness. One is perfect harmony; the other produces strife. One is the higher tide of the Spirit; the other is earthly. One gets into the bliss of the presence of heaven; the other never rises from earthly associations.

Claim your right; claim your position. The person who asks for a gift twice will never get it under any circumstances. I am not moved by what you think about it. I believe this is sovereign from God's altar. You never get a gift if you ask for it twice. But God will have mercy upon you if you stop asking and believe.

There is not a higher order that God puts in motion with a person who believes than this: *"Ask, and you will receive"* (John 16:24). If you dare to ask for any gift, if you really believe that it is a necessary gift, if you dare to ask and will not move from it but begin to act in it, you will find that the gift is there.

If you want to be in the will of God, you will have to be stubborn. What do I mean by this? I mean that you will have to be unchangeable. Do you think that if you get a gift, you will feel it? It is nothing like that. If you ask for a gift, do not expect that there will be a feeling with it. There is something better; there is a fact with it, and the fact will bring the feeling after the manifestation. People want feelings for gifts. There is no such thing. You will make the biggest mistake if you dare to continue praying about anything until you feel like doing something. As sure as can be, you have lost your faith. You have to believe that after you receive, you have the power, and that you begin to act in the power.

The morning after I received the gift of tongues, I went out of the house with a box of tools on my back; I was going down the street to do some work. The power of God lit me up and I broke out in tongues—loudly. My, they were loud! The street was filled with people, and there were some gardeners trimming some hedges and cutting the grass. When they heard me, they stuck their heads over the hedges, looking as if they had swan necks.

"Whatever is up? Why, it is the plumber."

I said, "Lord, I am not responsible for this, and I won't go from this place until I have the interpretation."

God knows that I wouldn't have moved from that place. And out came the interpretation:

Over the hills and far away before the brink of day, the Lord your God will send you forth and prosper all your way.

59

This is the point: the gift was there. I did not pray for it. I did not say, "Lord, give me the interpretation." I said, "If you don't give it to me, I won't move." By this I meant that I was determined to have the gift.

It has been surprising, but at every place where I am, the Spirit of the Lord moves upon me.

I want to say something about the gift of interpretation because it is so sublime, it is so divine, it is such a union with the Christ. It is a pleasing place with the Christ. It is not the Holy Spirit who is using it so much, but it is the Christ who is to be glorified in that act, for the Trinity moves absolutely collectively in the body.

As soon as that incident had taken place, wherever I went, when anybody spoke in tongues, I did not say, "Lord, give me the interpretation." That would have been wrong. I lived in a fact. Now, what is a fact? A fact is what produces. Fact produces; fact has it. Faith is a fact. Faith moves fear and faction. Faith is audacity. Faith is a personality. Faith is the living Christ manifested in the believer.

Now, what is interpretation? Interpretation moves and brings forth the words of God without the person thinking about it. If you get words before you have received from God, that is not interpretation. The person who interprets does not have the words. The gift breathes forth, and the person speaks, never stopping until he is through. He does not know what he is going to say until the words are out. He does not form them; he does not plan them. Interpretation is a divine flood, just as tongues are a flood. So it requires continual faith to produce this thing.

A divine gift has divine comprehension. It is also full of prophetic utterances. There is no such thing as an end to the divine vocabulary.

What is faith? Is it a pledge? It is more than that. Is it a present? It is more than that. It is relationship. Now, is there something better than relationship? Yes. What is it? Sonship is relationship, but heirship is closer still; and faith is *"God... manifested in the flesh"* (1 Tim. 3:16).

"What was Jesus?" you ask.

Jesus was the glory manifested in human incarnation.

"Was He anything else?"

Yes. Jesus was the fullness of the *"express image"* of the Father (Heb. 1:3). Is that fullness ours? Yes. Who are the chosen ones? They are those who ask and believe and see it done. God will make you chosen if you believe it.

Let us repent of everything that is hindering us; let us give place to God. Let us lose ourselves in Him. Let us have no self-righteousness, but let us have brokenness, humbleness, submission. Oh, may there be such brokenheartedness in us today! May we be dead indeed and alive indeed with refreshing from the presence of the Most High God!

Some of you have been saying, "Oh, I wish I could know how to get a gift." Some of you have felt the striving of the Holy Spirit within you. Oh, beloved, rise to the occasion this day. Believe God. Ask God for gifts, and it may come to pass in your life. But do not ask unless you know it is the desire of your heart. God grant to us gifts and graces!

SIX

THE WORD OF WISDOM

*For to one is given the word of wisdom
through the Spirit.*
—1 Corinthians 12:8

od bless you! When He blesses, no one can curse. When God is with you, it is impossible for anyone to be against you (Rom. 8:31). When God has put His hand upon you, every way will open with blessing to others. The greatest thing that God has allowed us to come into is the plan of distributing His blessing to others.

"I will bless you and...you shall be a blessing" (Gen. 12:2). When we know the power of almighty God, we never need to be afraid of any weapon that is formed against us (Isa. 54:17), believing that the Lord of Hosts will rise up and stand against the enemy. *"The LORD will cause your enemies who rise against you to be defeated before your face; they shall come out against you one way and flee before you seven ways"* (Deut. 28:7).

God's power upon us, His wonderful blessing of us, His providential promise written down for us are to make us ready, every day and under all circumstances, to know that He who promised will surely fulfill.

63

What a wonderful Christ! God has chosen a blessing for us in the midst of anything we encounter. The power of the Highest overshadows us, the glory of the Lord is behind us and before us. Who is able to withstand that almightiness!

God, breathe upon us so that we may be *"endued with power from on high"* (Luke 24:49), enriched with all the enrichment of heaven, crowned with blessing.

The Lord will lead us forth from victory to victory as His people. Oh, what a blessing to know that we are the fruit of the Lord! His people are the precious fruit of the earth.

I am not afraid to say these things to you because I know God wants to bless you. Why should you go away without blessing when God has promised that you will have a portion that cannot be measured (John 3:34)? Why should you fear when God wants to remove fear?

Are you ready? You say, "What for?" Oh, for His blessing that will fill your life, overflow you, change you.

Are you ready? Ready for what? To get a childlike simplicity and to look into the face of the Father and believe that all His promises are *"Yes"* and *"Amen"* (2 Cor. 1:20) to you.

Are you ready? Ready for what? To be awakened into that *"Spirit of adoption"* (Rom. 8:15) that believes all things and dares to ask the Father.

SPIRITUAL GIFTS

We have carefully gone through a few verses in the twelfth chapter of 1 Corinthians, so I hope you are well established in the thought that you are not to be ignorant about the gifts of the Holy Spirit. God does not intend for you to be ignorant concerning spiritual gifts: gifts that have revelation, that have divine knowledge, that have within them the power to deliver others and the power to pray through.

The gift of intercession, the gift of laying hands on the sick, the gift of prophecy, the gift of the word of wisdom, the gift of the word of knowledge, the gift of discerning spirits, the gift of tongues, and the gift of interpretation—all these are included in this one verse: *"Now concerning spiritual gifts, brethren, I do not want you to be ignorant"* (1 Cor. 12:1).

So I implore you to think seriously in your heart—because you have to be in the world but not of it—that you need to be a personal manifestation of the living Christ. Just as Christ walked about the earth, you have to walk about as a child of God, with power and manifestation. People do not take time to read the Bible, so you have to be a walking epistle, *"known and read by all men"* (2 Cor. 3:2).

Seeing that this is so and that you have to correctly comprehend that Jesus is the Word and that you have to believe the Word of God and not change it because of people who have other opinions, take the Word of God. Yes, take the Word of God; it will furnish you as you stand strong in the Lord. It is there that you will find out that you do not need anything better; there is nothing better. It is there that you will find all you need: food for hunger, light for darkness, largeness of heart, conceptions of thought, and inspiration.

I like the words of Paul. They are beautiful, and they come forth so often by the power of the Spirit, such as this word: *"Strengthened with might through His Spirit in the inner man"* (Eph. 3:16). This might of the Spirit can fill everybody, and it brings forth the revelation of the Word.

THE GIVER, THEN GIFTS

We have clearly seen, I believe, why gifts were particularized, why there are varieties of gifts and varieties of positions in which to hold gifts. We must not forget that the Giver is to be received before the gifts.

Salvation always precedes sanctification, and sanctification will always precede the baptism of the Holy Spirit. Sanctification prepares the body for the Holy Spirit, and when the body is rightly prepared for the Spirit, then it is the work of Jesus to baptize with the Holy Spirit.

The Holy Spirit then makes Jesus King in your life; you regard Him as Lord and Master over all things, and you become submissive to Him in all things. You are not afraid to say, "You are mine! I love You!"

I love Him. He is so beautiful; He is so sweet; He is so loving; He is so kind! He never turns a deaf ear; He never leaves you in distress. He heals brokenheartedness; He liberates the captive; and for those who are down and out, He comes right into that place and lifts the burden.

It is truly said of Him, "He came to His own and His own had no room for Him; but to as many as had room for Him, He gave them power to become the sons of God." (See John 1:11–12.)

Thus I bring you again to the nature of sonship: it is grace bestowed, poured out, pressed through, or covering you, preserving you from all evil. It is boundless grace, grace that brings capability for your lack of ability, until God has you in His own mind and purpose.

THE GIFT OF THE WORD OF WISDOM

In 1 Corinthians 12:8, the Word of God tells us about the word of wisdom: *"For to one is given the word of wisdom through the Spirit."* It does not say—and you must clearly understand it—it does not say "the gift of wisdom" but the gift of *"the word of wisdom."* You have to *"rightly* [handle] *the word of truth"* (2 Tim. 2:15) because it will mean so much to us.

The gift of the word of wisdom is necessary in many instances. For example, when you want to build another church building, maybe larger than the one you are in, so that everybody can speak and be heard without any trouble, a word of wisdom is needed regarding how to build the place for God's service.

A word of wisdom is necessary when you are faced with a choice and it is difficult for you to know in what direction to go. That word can come to you in a moment and prepare you for the right way.

The gift of the word of wisdom is meant for a needy hour when you are under great stress concerning some business transaction; provided it is a godly transaction, you can ask God what to do and you will receive wisdom along two lines.

It may come through the gift of the word of wisdom, or it may come forth just because the power of the Holy Spirit is upon you. I have been trying to show you that if you are filled with the Holy Spirit, the Holy Spirit can manifest any gift. At the same time, you are not to forget that the Word of God urges you to desire earnestly the best gifts; so while the best gift might be to you the word of wisdom, or some other gift, you should not be lacking in any gift.

That is a remarkable statement for me to make, but I declare to you that Scripture lends itself to me to be extravagant. When God speaks to me He says, "Anything you ask." (See John 15:7.) When God is speaking of the world's salvation He says, "Whosoever believes." (See John 3:16.) So I have an extravagant God with extravagant language to make me an extravagant person—in wisdom.

If you have extravagance without wisdom, you will know very well that it is going to be of no profit. You have to learn not to be extravagant in this way so that you will not waste anything, and you have to learn above all things that you have to be out and God has to be in. The trouble with so many people is that they have never gotten out so He could get in. But if God ever gets in, you will first have gotten out, never to come in anymore.

To this end, we pray that God will show us now why we really need the word of wisdom and how we may be in a place in which we will surely know it is of God. I am going to give you an example of the word of wisdom through an experience I had, and it will help you more than anything else.

A QUESTIONABLE WORD AND A WORD OF WISDOM

One day I went out of my house and saw a friend of mine named John who lived opposite me. He crossed the road, came up to me, and said, "Now, Smith, how are you?"

"Very well, John," I said.

"Well," he said, "my wife and I have been thinking and praying and talking together about selling our house, and every time we think about it in any way, your name is the only one we think about."

That was a strange thing to me.

"Will you buy it?" he asked.

Now, if you remember, when David went wrong he only went wrong because he violated the holy communion and knowledge of what kept him. What was it? What was the word that would have saved him? *"You shall not covet your neighbor's wife"* (Exod. 20:17). He had to break that law to commit sin.

I was not dealing with a sin; however, looking back, I see that there were many questionable things about the situation, so that if I had thought about it for a moment, I would have been saved from many weeks of brokenheartedness and sorrow.

What was the first thing that I should have asked myself? "Can I live in two houses? No. Well, then, one is sufficient."

The next thing was, "Do I have the money to buy the house? No."

That is sufficient in itself, for God does not want any person to be in debt, and when you learn that secret, it will save you from thousands of sleepless nights. But I was like many people; we are all learning, and none of us is perfect. However, I do thank God that we are called to perfection, whether we come into it at once or not. If you miss the mark of holiness ten times a day, fortify yourself to believe that God intends for you to be holy, and then stand again. Do not give in when you miss the mark.

There is a saying that goes something like this: "No man fails to succeed in life because he makes a blunder; it is when he makes the blunder twice." No person who fails once loses his *"high calling"* (Phil. 3:14 KJV). Therefore, the Word of God says that when you repent with godly repentance, you will never do the same thing again. (See 2 Corinthians 7:9–11.)

It is not for you to give in; you have to fortify yourself. The day is young; the opportunities are tremendously large. May God help you not to give in. Believe that God can make you new and turn you into another person.

Now, what was the trouble with me? It was that I didn't discuss this transaction with God. Many of you are in the same place. What do we do afterward? We begin working our way out. So I began working this thing out.

"How much will you take for it?" I asked.

He named the price. I thought to myself—this was a human thought—"Now, the banking society will give me all I want. They are well acquainted with me; that will be no trouble."

So the loan officer came to look over the house.

"It is a beautiful house," he said. "It is very reasonable. You will lose nothing on this if you ever sell it. It is well worth the money. But I cannot give you within five hundred dollars of what you need."

I did not have five hundred dollars; I couldn't get it out of the business I had at that time, so I still tried a human way. I did not go to God. If I had, I could have gotten out of it. But I tried to work my way out. Why? Because I knew I was wrong from the beginning.

The first thing I did was to try my relatives. Have you ever done that? What was wrong? They were all so pleased to see me, but I was either a bit too soon or a little bit too late; I absolutely just missed it. They all wanted to lend me the money, but I was there at the wrong time. I tell you, every time I saw a relative, I had a Turkish bath without paying for it.

I had another human plan then: I tried my friends. The same thing happened.

Then I went to my lovely wife. Oh, she was a darling! She was holy! I went to her and I said, "Oh, Mother, I am in a hard place."

"I know," she said. "I will tell you what you have never done, my dear."

"What?"

"You have never gone to God once about this thing."

That is the secret. When you get out of the will of God, then you try your own way.

So then I knew she knew, and I knew what I would get if I went to prayer.

"All right, my dear, I will go pray."

It is lovely to have a place to go in which to pray—those places where you open your eyes to see if you can see Him in reality because He is so near. Ah, to walk with God!

"Father," I said, "You know all about it. If you will forgive me this time, I will never trouble you again as long as I live with anything like this."

And then came the word of wisdom. He has it. And yet it was the most ridiculous word I ever heard in all my life. The Lord said, "Go see Brother Webster."

I came downstairs. I said, "He has spoken."

"I knew He would."

"Yes, but you see He said such a ridiculous thing."

71

"Believe it," she said. "It will be all right. When God speaks, you know it means it is all right."

"But Mother, you could hardly think it could be right. He has told me to go see Brother Webster."

"Go," she said.

Brother Webster was a man who kilned lime. The most he ever got per week, to my knowledge, was $3.50. He wore corduroy trousers and a pair of big work boots. But he was a godly man.

Early in the morning, I jumped onto my bicycle and went to his house. I got there at eight o'clock.

"Why, Brother Wigglesworth, what brings you so early?" he asked.

"I was speaking to the Lord last night about a little trouble," I said, "and He told me to come and see you."

"If that is the case," he said, "we will go down to my house and talk to the Lord."

We went to the house and he locked the door.

"Now, tell me," he said.

"Well, three weeks ago I arranged to buy a house. I found out I was short five hundred dollars. I have tried everything I know and have failed. My wife told me last night to go to God, and while I was there God said, 'Go see Brother Webster,' so here I am."

"How long have you needed it?"

"Three weeks."

"And you have never come to see me before?"

"No, God never told me."

I could have been able to know the next day if I had gone to God, but I tried my way and went to every man possible without going straight to God. I hope you won't do that now that you are to have the word of wisdom God is going to give you.

Brother Webster said to me, "For twenty years I have been putting aside a little more than half a dollar a week into a cooperative society. Three weeks ago they told me that I had five hundred dollars and that I must take it out because I was not doing business with them. I brought it home. I put it under the mattresses, under the floor boards, in the ceiling, everywhere. Oh, I have been so troubled by it! If it will do you any good, you can have it."

> He knows it all, He knows it all,
> My Father knows it all;
> Your bitter tears, how oft they flow,
> He knows, my Father knows it all.

I would like to change that verse somewhat. I will sing it the way God changed it for me:

> He knows it all, He knows it all,
> My Father knows it all;
> The joy that comes and overflows,
> He knows, my Father sends it all.

Yes, He knows. Glory to God!

"I had so much trouble," Brother Webster said, "that I took it to the bank yesterday to get rid of it. If I can get it out today, you can have it."

He went to the bank and asked, "How much can I have?"

"Why, it is your own," they said. "You can have it all."

He came out, gave it to me, and said, "There it is! If it is as much blessing to you as it has been trouble to me, you will have a lot of blessing."

Yes, beloved, He knows just what you need. Don't you know that if I had gone to the right place right away, I would never have been in trouble? What I ought to have known was this: there was no need for the house at all.

I could not rest. I got rid of the house and took the money back to Brother Webster and said, "Take it back; take the money back. It will be trouble to me if I keep that money; take it."

Oh, to be in the will of God!

Don't you see, beloved, there is the word, the word of wisdom. One word is sufficient; you don't need a lot. One little word from God is all you require. You can count on it; it will never fail. It will bring forth what God has desired.

May the Lord give wisdom to you so that you may *"rightly* [handle] *the word of truth"* (2 Tim. 2:15), walk in the *"fear of the LORD"* (2 Chron. 19:7), and be an example to other believers (1 Tim. 4:12). Never take advantage of the Holy Spirit, but allow the Holy Spirit to take advantage of you.

I have come to a conclusion that is very beautiful, in my estimation. I once thought I possessed the Holy Spirit, but I have come to the conclusion that He has to be entirely the Possessor of me.

God can tame your tongue. God can so reserve you for Himself that your entire body will be operating in the Spirit.

INTERPRETATION OF TONGUES
The Lord of Hosts is in the place, waiting to change the human race and fit it for a heavenly place.

74

SEVEN

THE WORD OF KNOWLEDGE AND THE GIFT OF FAITH

To another [is given] *the word of knowledge through the same Spirit, to another faith by the same Spirit.*
—1 Corinthians 12:8–9

e have not passed this way before. I believe that Satan has many devices and that they are worse today than ever before. But I also believe that there is to be a full manifestation on the earth of the power and glory of God to defeat every device of Satan.

In Ephesians 4 we are told to endeavor *"to keep the unity of the Spirit in the bond of peace,"* for *"there is one body and one Spirit...one Lord, one faith, one baptism; one God and Father of all"* (vv. 3–6). The baptism of the Spirit is to make us all one. Paul told us that *"by one Spirit we were all baptized into one body...and have all been made to drink into one Spirit"* (1 Cor. 12:13). It is God's intention that we speak the same thing. If we all have the full revelation of the Spirit of God, we will all see the same thing. Paul asked the Corinthians, *"Is Christ divided?"* (1 Cor. 1:13). When the Holy Spirit has full control, Christ is never divided. His body is not divided; there is no division. Schism and division are products of the carnal mind.

THE WORD OF KNOWLEDGE

How important it is that we have the manifestation of *"the word of knowledge"* in our midst. The same Spirit who brings forth the word of wisdom brings forth the word of knowledge. The revelation of the mysteries of God comes by the Spirit, and we must have a supernatural word of knowledge in order to convey to others the things that the Spirit of God has revealed. The Spirit of God reveals Christ in all His wonderful fullness, and He shows Him to us from the beginning to the end of the Scriptures. It is the Scriptures that make us *"wise for salvation"* (2 Tim. 3:15) and that open to us the depths of the kingdom of heaven, revealing all of the divine mind to us.

There are thousands of people who read and study the Word of God. But it is not quickened to them. The Bible is a dead letter except by the Spirit. The words that Christ spoke were not just dead words, but they were spirit and life (John 6:63). And so it is the intention of God that a living word, a word of truth, the word of God, a supernatural word of knowledge will come forth from us through the power of the Spirit of God. It is the Holy Spirit who will bring forth utterances from our lips and a divine revelation of all the mind of God.

The child of God ought to thirst for the Word. He should know nothing else but the Word, and he should know nothing among men except Jesus (1 Cor. 2:2). *"Man shall not live by bread alone, but by every word that proceeds from the mouth of God"* (Matt. 4:4). It is as we feed on the Word and meditate on the message it contains that the Spirit of God can vitalize what we have received and bring forth through us the word of knowledge. This word will be as full of power and life as when He, the Spirit of God, moved upon holy men in ancient times and gave them the inspired Scriptures. All the Scriptures were inspired by God (2 Tim. 3:16) as they came forth at the beginning, and through the same Spirit they should come forth from us vitalized, *"living and powerful, and sharper than any two-edged sword"* (Heb. 4:12).

With the gifts of the Spirit should come the fruit of the Spirit. With wisdom we should have love, with knowledge we should have joy, and with faith we should have the fruit of peace. Faith is always accompanied by peace. Faith always rests. Faith laughs at impossibilities. Salvation is by faith, through grace, and *"it is the gift of God"* (Eph. 2:8).

THE POWER OF FAITH

We are kept by the power of God through faith. God gives faith, and nothing can take it away. By faith we have power to enter into the wonderful things of God. There are three kinds of faith: saving faith, which is the gift of God; the faith of the Lord Jesus; and the gift of faith. You will remember the word that the Lord Jesus Christ gave to Paul, to which he referred in Acts 26, where the Lord commissioned him to go to the Gentiles:

To open their eyes, in order to turn them from darkness to light, and from the power of Satan to God, that they may receive forgiveness of sins and an inheritance among those who are sanctified by faith in Me. (Acts 26:18)

Oh, this wonderful faith of the Lord Jesus. Our faith comes to an end. Many times I have been to the place where I have had to tell the Lord, "I have used all the faith I have," and then He has placed His own faith within me.

One of my fellow workers in ministry said to me at Christmastime, "Wigglesworth, I was never so near the end of my finances in my life." I replied, "Thank God, you are just at the opening of God's treasures." It is when we are at the end of our own resources that we can enter into the riches of God's resources. It is when we possess nothing that we can possess all things. The Lord will always meet you when you are on the edge of living.

I was in Ireland one time, and I went to a house and said to the lady who came to the door, "Is Brother Wallace here?" She replied, "Oh, he has gone to Bangor, but God has sent you here for me. I need you. Come in." She told me her husband was a deacon of the Presbyterian church. She herself had received the baptism of the Spirit while she was a member of the Presbyterian church, but they did not accept it as from God. The people of the church said to her husband, "This thing cannot go on. We don't want you to be a deacon any longer, and your wife is not wanted in the church."

The man was very enraged, and he became incensed against his wife. It seemed as though an evil spirit had possessed him, and the home that had once been peaceful became very terrible. Finally, he left home without leaving behind any money for his wife. The woman asked me what she should do.

We went to prayer, and before we had prayed five minutes, the woman was mightily filled with the Holy Spirit. I said to her, "Sit down and let me talk to you. Are you often in the Spirit like this?" She said, "Yes, and what could I do without the Holy Spirit now?" I said to her, "The situation is yours. The Word of God says that you have power to sanctify your husband. (See 1 Corinthians 7:14.) Dare to believe the Word of God. Now the first thing we must do is to pray that your husband comes back tonight." She said, "I know he won't." I replied, "If we agree together, it is done." She said, "I will agree." Then I said to her, "When he comes home, show him all possible love; lavish everything upon him. If he won't hear what you have to say, let him go to bed. The situation is yours. Get down before God and claim him for the Lord. Get into the glory just as you have gotten into it today, and as the Spirit of God prays through you, you will find that God will grant all the desires of your heart."

A month later I saw this sister at a conference. She told how her husband came home that night. He went to bed, but she prayed right through to victory and then put her hands on him and prayed. He cried out for mercy. The Lord saved him and baptized him in the Holy Spirit. The power of God is beyond all our conception. The trouble is that we do not have the power of God in a full manifestation because of our finite thoughts, but as we go on and let God have His way, there is no limit to what our limitless God will do in response to a limitless faith. But you will never get anywhere unless you are in constant pursuit of all the power of God.

One day when I came home from our open-air meeting at eleven o'clock, I found that my wife was out. I asked, "Where is she?" I was told that she was down at Mitchell's. I had seen Mitchell that day and knew that he was at the point of death. I knew that it would be impossible for him to survive the day unless the Lord undertook to heal him.

There are many who let up in sickness and do not take hold of the life of the Lord Jesus Christ that is provided for them. For example, I was taken to see a woman who was dying, and I said to her, "How are things with you?" She answered, "I have faith; I believe." I said, "You know that you do not have faith. You know that you are dying. It is not faith that you have; it is language." There is a difference between language and faith. I saw that she was in the hands of the Devil. There was no possibility of life until he was removed from the premises. I hate the Devil, and I laid hold of the woman and shouted, "Come out, you demon of death. I command you to come out in the name of Jesus." In one minute she stood on her feet in victory.

But to return to the case of Brother Mitchell, I hurried down to the house, and as I got near I heard terrible screams. I knew that something had happened. I saw Mrs. Mitchell on the staircase and asked, "What is up?" She replied, "He is gone! He is gone!" I just passed by her and went into the room. Immediately I saw that Mitchell had gone. I could not understand it, but I began to pray. My wife was always afraid that I would go too far, and she laid hold of me and said, "Don't, Dad! Don't you see that he is dead?" I continued to pray and my wife continued to cry out to me, "Don't, Dad. Don't you see that he is dead?" But I continued praying. I got as far as I could with my own faith, and then God laid hold of me. Oh, it was such a laying hold that I could believe for anything. The faith of the Lord Jesus laid hold of me, and a solid peace came into my heart. I shouted, "He lives! He lives! He lives!" And he is living today.

There is a difference between our faith and the faith of the Lord Jesus. The faith of the Lord Jesus is needed. We must change faith from time to time. Your faith may get to a place where it wavers. The faith of Christ never wavers. When you have His faith, the thing is finished. When you have that faith, you will never look at things as they are. You will see the things of nature give way to the things of the Spirit; you will see the temporal swallowed up in the eternal.

I was at a camp meeting in Cazadero, California, about eight years ago, and a remarkable thing happened. A man came who was stone deaf. I prayed for him, and I knew that God had healed him. Then came the test. He would always move his chair up to the platform, and every time I got up to speak, he would get up as close as he could and strain his ears to catch what I had to say. The Devil said, "It isn't done." I declared, "It is done." This went on for three weeks, and then the manifestation came. He could hear distinctly from sixty yards away. When his ears were opened, he thought it was so great that he had to stop the meeting and tell everybody about it. I met him in Oakland recently and he was hearing perfectly. As we remain steadfast and unmovable on the ground of faith, we will see in perfect manifestation what we are believing for.

THE GIFT OF FAITH

People say to me, "Do you not have the gift of faith?" I say that it is an important gift, but that what is still more important is for us to be making an advancement in God every moment. Looking at the Word of God, I find that its realities are greater to me today than they were yesterday. It is the most sublime, joyful truth that God brings an enlargement, always an enlargement. There is nothing dead, dry, or barren in this life of the Spirit; God is always moving us on to something higher, and as we move on in the Spirit, our faith will always rise to the occasion as different circumstances arise.

This is how the gift of faith is manifested. You see something, and you know that your own faith is nothing in the situation. The other day I was in San Francisco. I was sitting on a streetcar, and I saw a boy in great agony on the street. I said, "Let me get out." I rushed to where the boy was. He was in agony because of stomach cramps. I put my hand on his stomach in the name of Jesus. The boy jumped and stared at me with astonishment. He found himself instantly free of pain. The gift of faith dared in the face of everything. It is as we are in the Spirit that the Spirit of God will operate this gift anywhere and at any time.

When the Spirit of God is operating this gift within a person, He causes him to know what God is going to do. When the man with the withered hand was in the synagogue, Jesus got all the people to look to see what would happen. The gift of faith always knows the results. Jesus said to the man, *"Stretch out your hand"* (Matt. 12:13). His word had creative force. He was not living on the edge of speculation. He spoke and something happened. He spoke at the beginning, and the world came into being. He speaks today, and things such as I have just described have to come to pass. He is the Son of God, and He came to bring us into sonship. He was the *"firstfruits"* of the Resurrection (1 Cor. 15:20), and He calls us to be *"firstfruits"* (James 1:18), to be the same kind of fruit as Himself.

There is an important point here. You cannot have the gifts by mere human desire. The Spirit of God distributes them *"to each one individually as He wills"* (1 Cor. 12:11). God cannot trust some people with a gift, but those who have a humble, broken, contrite heart He can trust (Isa. 66:2).

One day I was in a meeting where there were a lot of doctors and eminent men and many ministers. It was at a conference, and the power of God fell on the meeting. One humble little girl who served as a waitress opened her being to the Lord and was immediately filled with the Holy Spirit and began to speak in tongues. All these big men stretched their necks and looked up to see what was happening. They were saying, "Who is it?" Then they learned it was "the servant." Nobody received except the servant! These things are hidden and kept back from the *"wise and prudent"* (Matt. 11:25), but the little children, the humble ones, are the ones who receive. We cannot have faith if we show undue deference to one another. A man who is going on with God won't accept honor from his fellow beings. God honors the man who has a broken, contrite spirit. How can I get to that place?

So many people want to do great things and to be seen doing them, but the one whom God will use is the one who is willing to be told what to do. My Lord Jesus never said He could do things, but He did them. When that funeral procession was coming up from Nain with the widow's son being carried in an open coffin, Jesus made them lay the coffin down. (See Luke 7:11–14.) He spoke the word, *"Arise"* (v. 14), and gave the son back to the widow. He had compassion for her. And you and I will never do anything except along the lines of compassion. We will never be able to remove the cancer until we are immersed so deeply in the power of the Holy Spirit that the compassion of Christ is moving through us.

I find that in everything my Lord did, He said that He did not do it but that Another who was in Him did the work (John 14:10). What a holy submission! He was just an instrument for the glory of God. Have we reached a place where we dare to be trusted with the gift? I see in 1 Corinthians 13 that if I have faith to move mountains and do not have love, all is a failure. When my love is so deepened in God that I only move for the glory of God, then the gifts can be made manifest. God wants to be manifested and to manifest His glory to those who are humble.

A faint heart can never have a gift. Two things are essential: first, love; and secondly, determination—a boldness of faith that will cause God to fulfill His Word.

When I was baptized in the Holy Spirit, I had a wonderful time and had utterances in the Spirit, but for some time afterward, I did not again speak in tongues. One day, as I was ministering to another, the Lord again gave me utterances in the Spirit. After this, I was going down the road one day and speaking in tongues a long while. There were some gardeners doing their work, and they stuck their heads out over the hedges to see what was going on. I said, "Lord, You have something new for me. You said that when a man speaks in tongues, he should ask for the interpretation. I ask for the interpretation, and I'll stay right here until I get it." And from that hour, the Lord has given me interpretation.

One time I was in Lincolnshire in England and came in touch with the old rector of the church there. He became very interested in what I had to say, and he asked me into his library. I never heard anything sweeter than the prayer the old man uttered as he got down to pray. He began to pray, "Lord, make me holy. Lord, sanctify me." I called out, "Wake up! Wake up now! Get up and sit in your chair." He sat up and looked at me. I said to him, "I thought you were holy." He answered, "Yes." "Then what makes you ask God to do what He has already done for you?" He began to laugh and then to speak in tongues. Let us move into the realm of faith and live in the realm of faith and let God have His way.

EIGHT

GIFTS OF HEALING AND THE WORKING OF MIRACLES

To another [are given] *the gifts of healing by the same Spirit; to another the working of miracles.*
—1 Corinthians 12:9–10 (KJV)

od has given us much in these last days, and where much is given, much will be required (Luke 12:48). The Lord has said to us:

You are the salt of the earth; but if the salt loses its flavor, how shall it be seasoned? It is then good for nothing but to be thrown out and trampled underfoot by men.   (Matt. 5:13)

Our Lord Jesus expressed a similar thought when He said, *"If anyone does not abide in Me, he is cast out as a branch and is withered; and they gather them and throw them into the fire, and they are burned"* (John 15:6). On the other hand, He told us, *"If you abide in Me, and My words abide in you, you will ask what you desire, and it shall be done for you"* (John 15:7).

If we do not move on with the Lord in these days, if we do not walk in the light of revealed truth, we will become as flavorless salt or a withered branch. This one thing we must do: *"Forgetting those things which are behind"*—both the past failures and the past blessings—we must reach forth for those things that are before us and *"press toward the mark for the prize of the high calling of God in Christ Jesus"* (Phil. 3:13–14 KJV).

For many years, the Lord has been moving me on and keeping me from spiritual stagnation. When I was in the Wesleyan Methodist Church, I was sure I was saved, and I was sure I was all right. The Lord said to me, "Come out," and I came out. When I was with the people known as the Brethren, I was sure I was all right then. But the Lord said, "Come out." Then I went into the Salvation Army. At that time, it was full of life, and there were revivals everywhere. But the Salvation Army went into natural things, and the great revivals that they had in those early days ceased. The Lord said to me, "Come out," and I came out. I have had to come out three times since. I believe that this Pentecostal revival that we are now in is the best thing that the Lord has on the earth today; and yet I believe that God will bring something out of this revival that is going to be still better. God has no use for anyone who is not hungering and thirsting for even more of Himself and His righteousness.

The Lord has told us to *"earnestly desire the best gifts"* (1 Cor. 12:31), and we need to earnestly desire those gifts that will bring Him the most glory. We need to see the gifts of healing and the working of miracles in operation today. Some say that it is necessary for us to have the gift of discernment in operation with the gifts of healing, but even apart from this gift, I believe that the Holy Spirit will have a divine revelation for us as we deal with the sick.

Most people think they have discernment; but if they would turn their discernment on themselves for twelve months, they would never want to "discern" again. The gift of discernment is not criticism. I am satisfied that in Pentecostal circles today, our paramount need is more perfect love.

Perfect love will never want the preeminence in everything; it will never want to take the place of another; it will always be willing to take the back seat. If you go to a Bible conference, there is always someone who wants to give a message, who wants to be heard. If you have a desire to go to a conference, you should have three things settled in your mind: Do I want to be heard? Do I want to be seen? Do I want anything on the line of finances? If I have these things in my heart, I have no right to be there.

The one thing that must move us is the constraining love of God to minister for Him. A preacher always loses out when he gets his mind on finances. It is advisable for Pentecostal preachers to avoid making much of finances except to stir people up to help support our missionaries financially. A preacher who gets big collections for the missionaries never needs to fear; the Lord will take care of his finances.

A preacher should not arrive at a place and say that God has sent him. I am always fearful when I hear a man advertising this. If he is sent by God, the believers will know it. God has His plans for His servants, and we must live in His plans so completely that He will place us where He wants us. If you seek nothing but the will of God, He will always put you in the right place at the right time.

I want you to see that the gifts of healing and the working of miracles are part of the Spirit's plan and will come forth in operation as we are working along that plan. I must know the movement of the Spirit and the voice of God. I must understand the will of God if I am to see the gifts of the Spirit in operation.

HEALING POWER

The people of the Holy Spirit have a ministry. Everyone who has received the Holy Spirit is so filled with the Spirit that, without having the specific gift of healing, the Holy Spirit within him may bring forth healing power.

That is the reason I say to you, "Never be afraid of coming near me when I am praying for the sick." I love to have people help me. Why? Because I know that there are people who have a very dim conception of what they have. I believe that the power of the Holy Spirit you have received has power to bring you into focus in such a way that you will dare to believe God for healing, apart from knowing you have a gift.

THE GIFTS OF HEALING

Now I will deal with the gift itself. It is actually *"gifts"* of healing, not the "gift" of healing. There is a difference, and we must give it the proper name. Gifts of healing can deal with every case of sickness, every disease that there is. These gifts are so full that they are beyond human expression, but you come into the fullness of them as the light brings revelation to you.

There is something about a divine healing meeting that may be different in some respects than other meetings. I have people continually coming to me and saying, "When you are preaching, I see a halo around you," or "When you are preaching, I have seen angels standing around you."

I hear these things from time to time, and I am thankful that people have such spiritual vision. I do not have that kind of vision; however, I have the express glory, the glory of the Lord, covering me, the intense inner working of His power, until every time I have stood before you, I have known that I have not had to choose the words I have spoken. The language has been chosen, the thoughts have been chosen, and I have been speaking in prophecy more than in any other way. So I know we have been in the school of the Holy Spirit in a great way.

The only vision I have had in a divine healing meeting is this: so often, when I have laid hands upon the people, I have seen two hands go before my hands. This has happened many, many times.

The person who has the gifts of healing does not look to see what is happening. You will notice that after I have finished ministering, many things are manifested, but they don't move me. I am not moved by anything I see.

The divine gifts of healing are so profound in the person who has them that there is no such thing as doubt, and there could not be; whatever happens could not change the person's opinion or thought or act. He expects the very thing that God intends him to have as he lays hands upon the seeker.

Wherever I go, the manifestation of divine healing is considerably greater in every way after I leave than when I am there. Why? It is God's plan for me. God has great grace over me. Wonderful things have been accomplished, and people have told me what happened when I was there, but these things were hidden from me. God has a reason why He hides things from me.

When I lay hands upon people for a specific thing, I tell you, that thing will take place. I believe it will be so, and I never turn my ears or my eyes from the fact. It has to be so.

The gift of divine healing is more than audacity; it is more than an unction. Those are two big things; however, the gift of healing is the solid fact of a divine nature within the person pressing forward the very nature and act of the Lord, as if He were there. We are in this place to glorify the Father, and the Father will be glorified in the Son since we are not afraid of taking action in this day.

The gift of healing is a fact. It is a production; it is a faith; it is an unwavering trust; it is a confidence; it is a reliability; it knows it will be.

People sometimes come to me very troubled. They say, "I had the gift of healing once, but something has happened and I do not have it now."

They never had it. *"The gifts and the calling of God are irrevocable"* (Rom. 11:29), and they remain under every circumstance except this: if you fall from grace and use a gift, it will work against you. If you use tongues out of the will of God, interpretation will condemn you. If you have been used and the gift has been exercised and then you have fallen from your high place, it will work against you.

MINISTERING HEALING

The gifts of healing are so varied. You may go to see ten people, and every case will be different. I am never happier in the Lord than when I am in a bedroom with a sick person. I have had more revelations of the Lord's presence when I have ministered to the sick at their bedsides than at any other time. It is as your heart goes out to the needy ones in deep compassion that the Lord manifests His presence. You are able to discern their conditions. It is then that you know you must be filled with the Spirit to deal with the conditions before you.

When people are sick, you frequently find that they are ignorant about Scripture. They usually know three Scriptures, though. They know about Paul's *"thorn in the flesh"* (2 Cor. 12:7); they know that Paul told Timothy to take *"a little wine"* for his *"stomach's sake"* (1 Tim. 5:23); and they know that Paul left someone sick somewhere, but they don't remember his name or the place, and they don't know in what chapter of the Bible it is found. (See 2 Timothy 4:20.) Most people think they have a thorn in the flesh. The chief thing in dealing with a person who is sick is to discern his exact condition. As you are ministering under the Spirit's power, the Lord will let you see just what will be the most helpful and the most faith-inspiring to him.

When I was in the plumbing business, I enjoyed praying for the sick. Urgent calls would come, and I would have no time to wash. With my hands all black, I would preach to these sick ones, my heart all aglow with love. Ah, your heart must be in it when you pray for the sick. You have to get right to the bottom of the cancer with a divine compassion, and then you will see the gifts of the Spirit in operation.

I was called at ten o'clock one night to pray for a young person who was dying of consumption and whom the doctor had given up on. As I looked, I saw that unless God intervened, it would be impossible for her to live. I turned to the mother and said, "Well, Mother, you will have to go to bed." She said, "Oh, I have not had my clothes off for three weeks." I said to the daughters, "You will have to go to bed," but they did not want to go. It was the same with the son. I put on my overcoat and said, "Goodbye, I'm leaving." They said, "Oh, don't leave us." I said, "I can do nothing here." They said, "Oh, if you will stay, we will all go to bed."

I knew that God would not move in an atmosphere of mere natural sympathy and unbelief. They all went to bed, and I stayed, and that was surely a time as I knelt by that bed face-to-face with death and the Devil. But God can change the hardest situation and make you know that He is almighty.

Then the fight came. It seemed as though the heavens were brass. I prayed from 11:00 P.M. to 3:30 A.M. I saw the glimmering light on the face of the sufferer and saw her pass away. The Devil said, "Now you are done for. You have come from Bradford, and the girl has died on your hands." I said, "It can't be. God did not send me here for nothing. This is a time to change strength." I remembered the passage that said, *"Men always ought to pray and not lose heart"* (Luke 18:1). Death had taken place, but I knew that my God was all-powerful and that He who had split the Red Sea is just the same today. It was a time when I would not accept "No" and God said "Yes."

I looked at the window, and at that moment, the face of Jesus appeared. It seemed as though a million rays of light were coming from His face. As He looked at the one who had just passed away, the color came back to her face. She rolled over and fell asleep. Then I had a glorious time. In the morning she woke early, put on a dressing gown, and walked to the piano. She started to play and to sing a wonderful song. The mother and the sister and the brother all came down to listen. The Lord had intervened. A miracle had been worked.

The Lord is calling us along this way. I thank God for difficult cases. The Lord has called us into heart union with Himself; He wants His bride to have one heart and one Spirit with Him and to do what He Himself loved to do. That case had to be a miracle. The lungs were gone; they were just in shreds. Yet the Lord restored her lungs, making them perfectly sound.

A fruit of the Spirit that must accompany the gift of healing is long-suffering. The man who is persevering with God to be used in healing must be a man of long-suffering. He must always be ready with a word of comfort. If the sick one is in distress and helpless and does not see everything eye to eye with you, you must bear with him. Our Lord Jesus Christ was filled with compassion and lived and moved in a place of long-suffering, and we will have to get into this place if we are to help needy ones.

There are some times when you pray for the sick, and you seem to be rough with them. But you are not dealing with a person; you are dealing with satanic forces that are binding the person. Your heart is full of love and compassion toward all; however, you are moved to a holy anger as you see the place the Devil has taken in the body of the sick one, and you deal with his position with a real forcefulness.

One day a pet dog followed a lady out of her house and ran all around her feet. She said to the dog, "My dear, I cannot have you with me today." The dog wagged its tail and made a big fuss. She said, "Go home, my dear." But the dog did not go. At last she shouted roughly, "Go home," and off it went. Some people deal with the Devil like that. The Devil can stand all the comfort you like to give him. Cast him out! You are not dealing with the person; you are dealing with the Devil. Demon power must be dislodged in the name of the Lord.

You are always right when you dare to deal with sickness as with the Devil. Much sickness is caused by some misconduct; there is something wrong, there is some neglect somewhere, and Satan has had a chance to get in. It is necessary to repent and confess where you have given place to the Devil (Eph. 4:27), and then he can be dealt with.

When you deal with a cancer case, recognize that a living evil spirit is destroying the body. I had to pray for a woman in Los Angeles one time who was suffering with cancer, and as soon as it was cursed, it stopped bleeding. It was dead. The next thing that happened was that the natural body pushed it out, because the natural body had no room for dead matter. It came out like a great big ball with tens of thousands of fibers. All these fibers had been pressing into the flesh. These evil powers move to get further hold of the body's system, but the moment they are destroyed, their hold is gone. Jesus told His disciples that He gave them power to loose and power to bind (Matt. 16:19). It is our privilege in the power of the Holy Spirit to loose the prisoners of Satan and to let the oppressed go free.

Take your position from the first epistle of John and declare, *"He who is in* [me] *is greater than he who is in the world"* (1 John 4:4). Then recognize that it is not you who has to deal with the power of the Devil, but the Greater One who is in you. Oh, what it means to be filled with Him! You can do nothing in yourself, but He who is in you will win the victory. Your being has become the temple of the Spirit. Your mouth, your mind, your whole being may be used and worked upon by the Spirit of God.

I was called to a certain town in Norway. The hall seated about fifteen hundred people. When I got to the place, it was packed, and hundreds were trying to get in. There were some policemen there. The first thing I did was to preach to the people outside the building. Then I said to the policemen, "It hurts me very much that there are more people outside than inside, and I feel I must preach to the people. I would like you to get me the marketplace to preach in." They secured a large park for me, and a big stand was erected, and I was able to preach to thousands.

After the preaching, we had some marvelous cases of healing. One man came a hundred miles, bringing his food with him. He had not been passing anything through his stomach for over a month because he had a large cancer on his stomach. He was healed at that meeting, and opening his package, he began eating for all the people to see.

There was a young woman there with a stiff hand. When she was a child, her mother, instead of making her use her arm, had allowed her to keep it dormant until it was stiff. This young woman was like the woman in the Bible who was bent over with the spirit of infirmity (Luke 13:11). As she stood before me, I cursed the spirit of infirmity in the name of Jesus. It was instantly cast out and the arm was free. Then she waved her hand all around.

At the close of the meeting, the Devil threw two people to the ground with fits. When the Devil is manifesting himself, then is the time to deal with him. Both of these people were delivered, and when they stood up and thanked and praised the Lord, what a wonderful time we had.

We need to wake up and strive to believe God. Before God could bring me to this place, He broke me a thousand times. I have wept; I have groaned. I have travailed many a night until God broke me. It seems to me that until God has mowed you down, you can never have this long-suffering for others. We will never have the gifts of healing and the working of miracles in operation unless we stand in the divine power that God gives us, unless we stand believing God and *"having done all"* (Eph. 6:13), we still stand believing.

We have been seeing wonderful miracles during these last days, and they are only a little of what we are going to see. I believe that we are on the threshold of wonderful things, but I want to emphasize that all these things will be only through the power of the Holy Spirit. You must not think that these gifts will fall upon you like ripe cherries. There is a sense in which you have to pay the price for everything you get. We must earnestly desire God's best gifts and say "Amen" to any preparation the Lord takes us through. In this way, we will be humble, useable vessels through whom He Himself can operate by means of the Spirit's power.

NINE

The Gift of Prophecy

To another [is given] *prophecy.*
—1 Corinthians 12:10

 want you to understand clearly that there are three kinds of prophecy. Get this in your heart, because Paul said, *"I wish you all spoke with tongues, but even more that you prophesied"* (1 Cor. 14:5).

Testimonial Prophecy

First, there is the prophecy that is the testimony of the saved person regarding what Jesus has done for him. Everyone, every newborn soul, has this kind of prophecy. Through the new birth that results in righteousness, God has given an anointing of the Spirit, a real unction of the Spirit of Christ. We felt when we were saved that we wanted everybody to be saved. That mindset has to be continuous; the whole world can be regenerated by the spirit of prophecy as we testify of our salvation in Christ. This kind of prophecy was described by an inhabitant of heaven to the apostle John in Revelation 19:10:

And I fell at his feet to worship him. But he said to me, "See that you do not do that! I am your fellow servant, and of your brethren who have the testimony of Jesus. Worship God! For the testimony of Jesus is the spirit of prophecy."

This is the same prophecy that Paul spoke about in 1 Corinthians 14:1: *"Pursue love, and desire spiritual gifts, but especially that you may prophesy."* This verse identifies prophecy as being more important than other gifts. Think about that: prophecy is to be chosen and desired above all the other gifts; the greatest among all the gifts is prophecy.

Why prophecy? Because prophecy by the power of the Spirit is the only power that saves humanity. We are told in the Word of God that the Gospel that is presented through prophecy has power to bring immortality and light. (See 2 Timothy 1:10.) Immortality is what abides forever. Light is what opens the understanding of your heart. Light and immortality come by the Gospel.

Prophecy is to be desired above all things, and every Christian has to have it. Every believer may have gifts, though there are very few who do; however, every believer has testimonial prophecy.

Now, from that same reference in Revelation 19:10, let us see what testimonial prophecy is and how it comes forth.

"I fell at his feet." Who is this inhabitant of heaven? The one speaking to John is a man who has been on the earth. Lots of people are foolishly led by the Devil to believe that after they die, their spirits will be asleep in the grave; this is absolutely contrary to the Word of God. Don't you know that even

if you live until the Lord comes, the body that you have must be put off and another must be put on, because you cannot go into heaven with your present body? Nothing makes you so foolish as to turn aside from the Word of God. If you ever want to be a fool, turn aside from the Word of God, and you will find yourself in a fool's paradise.

This man has been in the earth in the body and is now in heaven in the spirit, and he wants you to hear what he has to say: *"I am your fellow servant, and of your brethren who have the testimony of Jesus....For the testimony of Jesus is the spirit of prophecy"* (Rev. 19:10).

What is the testimony of Jesus? The testimony is: "Jesus has saved me." What the world wants to know today is how they can be saved.

Testify that you are saved. Your knees may knock together, you may be trembling as you do it, but when you get it out, you enter into the spirit of prophecy. Before you know where you are, you are saying things that the Spirit is saying.

There are thousands of Christians who have never received the baptism of the Holy Spirit but who have this wonderful spirit of prophecy. People are being saved everywhere by the testimony of such believers.

John Wesley was moved by the power of God, and he created revivals all over the world. After the people were saved, they testified.

If you cease from testifying, you will be sorry when you give an account of your life before God (Rom. 14:12). As you testify, you will be a vessel through which the power of God can bring salvation to people (1:16). Testify wherever you are.

103

INTERPRETATION OF TONGUES

"You have not chosen me, but I have chosen you and ordained you that you should go forth, your feet shod with the preparation of the Gospel of peace." What lovely feet! What lovely desire! A desire in your heart, because you are saved, to get everybody saved. The spirit of prophecy!

You must all preach from now on. Every one of you must be a preacher. You have a prophecy that has come from heaven to change you from vile inward corruption, to do away with your human, evil nature, and to put within you a spirit of testimony. You know that where once you were dead, behold, you are alive! (See Luke 15:24.)

INTERPRETATION OF TONGUES

Live in the place where the Lord your God moves you, not to go from house to house nor speak from person to person, but where the Lord directs you, for He has the person who is in need of truth waiting for watering with your watering can.

Oh, how the Lord wants to cheer you today! Do not forget that you are ambassadors for Christ (2 Cor. 5:20). Do not forget that you are now in the place where the prophets have a chance.

The Lord can bring you into a great place of splendor. He has His hand upon you. Whatever you do, desire to be holy, seek to be clean, so that you might always bear about in your body not only the dying of the Lord but also the life of the resurrection of the Lord (2 Cor. 4:10).

INTERPRETATION OF TONGUES

Lift up your hands and never be feeble, for the Lord has said, "Lift up holy hands." Don't be afraid of coming into the treasury, of making your hands clean, for they who bear the vessels of the Lord have to be only unto the Lord. So the Lord is bringing you to this great place of His pavilion so that He may clothe you upon with the Spirit, that your water will not fail. He will give you water and seed for your ministry, for remember, it is the same water and it is the same sower. So don't forget, beloved, you are coworkers together with Him, and your ministry in the Lord is not to be in vain. See to it that you live so that your seed is well watered.

Now, that is one kind of prophecy. General Booth, the founder of the Salvation Army, knew it. He got the vision as clear as anything from Wesley. The greatest revival that has ever swept the earth that we remember is the revival the Salvation Army brought.

God revealed Himself to Booth. Those who were saved testified. God moved the people who were saved—former drunkards and prostitutes—into the streets to prophesy in the Spirit of Jesus. This is the prophecy that you all have when you are saved. The spirit of prophecy is the testimony that you are saved by the blood of the Lamb.

ANOINTED PROPHECY

The next type of prophecy is given by the preacher who lives in anointing, in prophetic utterances. You will find that I mostly speak in prophecy.

Why? Well, it has pleased the Lord to bring me into this way of ministering so that I do not come to the platform with thought—that is, not with any thoughts of what I am going to say.

I want you to know another thing: I never say what I think. It is very much below a prophet of the Lord to begin to speak what he thinks to the people. The prophet must always say what he knows, because the people he is speaking to are the ones who have to think it out; but he is in the place of knowledge. The Holy Spirit takes the thoughts of Jesus and fills the prophet with divine life until he speaks divine utterances, until he knows.

Sometimes I speak quite a bit; I never take any thought at all concerning what I am speaking, but it flows out like rivers, prophecy of divine power. My natural makeup is not full, but my supernatural makeup is an overflowing full. I depend upon an overflowing full so that you may get something out of it, so that you also may be full to overflowing.

It is very important and very essential that the person who preaches should live in prophetic utterances. Then a preacher will never be lamentable in his divine position. He is standing before people as a chosen one of God. He is not in any way to preach anything unless he knows it is the Word of God, and there he is to be clothed with holiness like a garment of salvation.

Oh, this is true! The Spirit of the Lord is upon me now. I know it; I feel it. It is moving me; it chastens me; it is bringing me to a place where I know that if you listen, you will be blessed. The blessing of the Lord is upon you. Hear, for the Spirit speaks to you.

This is prophecy as the Spirit gives forth. It is the illumination of truth by the Word of Life. The Holy Spirit has the chief position in the place, taking words, actions, and everything else until the prophet stands there complete, the oracle of God, speaking words absolutely as if the Lord were here saying them.

These first two kinds of prophecy are divine inspiration, Holy Spirit utterances. In a very remarkable way by the Spirit of Jesus, every person can feel burnings and movings, chastenings and thrillings. It is wonderful. All you have to do is begin and you cannot stop.

There was something done on the cross that is truly wonderful. Don't you know you were made every bit whole? You were made holy; you were made a saint; you were absolutely cleansed from all unrighteousness. The new birth is a revelation of God in the soul. You are made His forever when you are saved by His power. No one can estimate the new birth; it is beyond all human power to estimate. The new birth is larger than our human capacities. And, thank God, we have touches from Him that make us on fire.

THE GIFT OF PROPHECY

We will now look at divine prophecy as a gift. I trust that many of you will have this gift.

This is the most wonderful of all prophecy and yet the most dangerous. There is a great deal of trouble in relation to the gift of prophecy; there always has been. So I want you to guard this gift. With the gift of prophecy, what you need to watch is this (it is the same with the gift of tongues and the gift of healing): even though the gift has been received and the people have been blessed through the gift, you are never to use the gift unless the power of the Spirit brings into you a great thirst and longing to do it. It would be a serious thing for me to speak in tongues at any moment just because I had the gift; without the unction of the Spirit, it would fall to nothing.

All gifts are of no account at all unless they are brought forth by the Giver of the gifts, and the Holy Spirit is the One who gives the nine gifts listed in 1 Corinthians 12. He brings anointing, fire, confirmation, and utterance, until those who hear are moved. When the Lord speaks, it changes and moves the natural, because it is supernatural. Supernatural always changes natural.

Prophecy is lovely because it makes the body very full of expressions of joy. It is lovely, for people all like to hear it. It is lovely when it is the Spirit moving.

Be careful when people are very pleased to hear you prophesy. Prophecy is like tongues; no man who speaks and speaks and speaks and speaks in tongues is to have control in a meeting. That is not what it means to have the advantage in a meeting. Having the advantage means that when the Spirit is upon you, you will speak in tongues, and you will close down the moment you know you are at the end. What spoils it is when people go on and on, and the hearers get tired of it because they want something that God can bring in and move quickly.

Don't think you will be heard by your *"many words"* (Matt. 6:7), either by tongues, prayer, or anything else. You are not heard because of your many words; you are heard because you are definite. All your spiritual abilities are going to be acceptable with others as you learn how to obey the Spirit and never to take advantage just because you are present in a meeting.

Here is another thing you have to learn: people rush up and down sometimes, and then they say to you, "Oh, I had to do that! I had to jump up and do that. I had to do that—and that—and that."

Don't believe them; it isn't true. There never was a person in the world, as long as he was in the body, who didn't have power over his spirit. And so, when people rush to you and say they have to do this, that, and the other, don't believe it. What are you to believe? You are to believe that when the Spirit is manifested in the order it should be, it will have three things with it: comfort, exhortation, and edification (1 Cor. 14:3).

If any of you find that I do not speak by the Spirit of God and teach the Scriptures only, which is what God desires, you meet me at the door and tell me. I have declared that this will be my constant purpose. I have declared that as long as I live, I will never exaggerate. Exaggeration is lying. What God wants is a people who are full of truth. I want God to so have you that your word will be your bond. Whenever you say anything, the people will be able to believe it; you have said it, and you will do it.

When the unction is upon you, when the power of God is manifested through you, one thing that will be accomplished by prophecy is comfort. The Holy Spirit can so have you in prophecy that all the people will be comforted.

But if you get away from that prophecy because you begin and the people are delighted, and if you go on until you come out with your own human words, you will lead people astray. People have been led to buy houses, to do all sorts of silly things, because of people who did not obey the Lord but brought in some human prophecy.

If anybody ever comes to you with human prophecy, say, "I know God, and unless God tells me, I won't move."

Don't be deluded by anybody. You can tell what is of the Lord. The Word of God distinctly says, *"Do not despise prophecies"* (1 Thess. 5:20). So whatever you do, do not despise them. However, in the next verse you are told to *"test all things"* (v. 21). Therefore, you may say, "Well now, if that is of the Lord, I will see if it corresponds to the Word of God." And you will have clear revelation as to whether it is the word of the Lord.

This is the day in which we need comforting, and the power of the Spirit can comfort you and send you away from these meetings knowing that you have been in the presence of God and have heard the Word of God.

There are people who, like Isaiah, have the gift of prophecy. Isaiah was so filled with this prophecy. He said, *"Unto us a Son is given"* (Isa. 9:6). This was definite, personal, truth, and knowledge. It took five hundred years to bring it to pass, but there it was, definitely declared beforehand:

> *And the government will be upon His shoulder. And His name will be called Wonderful, Counselor, Mighty God, Everlasting Father, Prince of Peace.* (v. 6)

Oh, hallelujah! All the way down through the Scriptures you will find such distinct prophecy. You will see the book of Isaiah filled with prophetic utterances. Begin with Genesis and go right through, and you will find the golden or the scarlet thread right through all the prophecies, declaring, "He is coming, He is coming! He is on the way; He will surely come!"

At the birth of Christ, the angels sang; the Babe was born. Prophecy was fulfilled!

And you shall call His name JESUS, for He will save His people from their sins.
(Matt. 1:21)

And this will be the sign to you: You will find a Babe wrapped in swaddling cloths, lying in a manger. (Luke 2:12)

Prophecy was also fulfilled in Jesus' crucifixion and resurrection:

You know that after two days is the Passover, and the Son of Man will be delivered up to be crucified. (Matt. 26:2)

As Moses lifted up the serpent in the wilderness, even so must the Son of Man be lifted up.
(John 3:14)

Ah, beloved, God can give you prophecy that will fulfill the past to a perfect degree, chapter and verse.

He is coming. Glory to God! The saints will be awakened; prophecy will appear. People will say, "Yes, He is coming; we know He is coming!"

And He will come!

111

TEN

THE DISCERNING
OF SPIRITS

To another [is given] *discerning of spirits.*
—1 Corinthians 12:10

iscernment is a very necessary gift to understand, and I want you to keep your mind clearly balanced about this. I want you to rightly divide this truth (2 Tim. 2:15), to keep clear in your mind what it is.

DISCERNMENT VERSUS JUDGING

In 1 Corinthians 12:10, it clearly says that there is a gift of *"discerning of spirits,"* but most people seem to think it is a discerning of human persons. It is amazing to find that all the people I come across— or most of them—seem to have a tremendous bent toward "discerning" others. If you carefully put this discerning of one another into real practice upon yourself for twelve months, you will never presume to try it upon another. You will see so many faults, so many crooked things about yourself, that you will say, "O God, make me right!"

There is a vast difference between natural discernment and spiritual discernment. This statement of Jesus is remarkable:

> *How can you say to your brother, "Let me remove the speck from your eye"; and look, a plank is in your own eye? Hypocrite! First remove the plank from your own eye, and then you will see clearly to remove the speck from your brother's eye.* (Matt. 7:4–5)

Remember that if you begin judging, it will lead you to judgment (vv. 1–2). If you begin using your discernment to weigh people by your standards, it will lead you to judgment. Ever since God showed me a certain passage in Romans 2, I have been very careful to examine myself before I begin judging:

> *Therefore you are inexcusable, O man, whoever you are who judge, for in whatever you judge another you condemn yourself; for you who judge practice the same things. But we know that the judgment of God is according to truth against those who practice such things. And do you think this, O man, you who judge those practicing such things, and doing the same, that you will escape the judgment of God?* (Rom. 2:1–3)

Balance that in your heart. It will save you from judging.

I have found that there are many notable people in the world, whom I have known personally, who have gotten to running another person down and finding fault. They are always faultfinding and judging people outright. I find that those people always fall in the mire. If I were to mention these people by name, you would know that what I am saying is true.

God save us from criticism! When we are pure in heart, we only think about pure things. When we are impure in heart, we speak and act and think as we are in our hearts. The pure in heart see purity. May God give us that inward desire for purity so that He can take away judging.

In the sixth chapter of Isaiah, we read of the prophet being in the presence of God. He found that even his lips were unclean, that everything was unclean (Isa. 6:5). But praise God, there is the same live coal for us today (vv. 6–7), the baptism of fire, the perfecting of the heart, the purifying of the mind, the regeneration of the spirit. How important it is that the fire of God touches our tongues!

Discerning Spirits

But it is the discerning of spirits that I want to talk about, as well as what to do when you have no discernment.

In 1 John 4:1 we are told, *"Beloved, do not believe every spirit, but test the spirits, whether they are of God."* We are further told:

> *And every spirit that does not confess that Jesus Christ has come in the flesh is not of God. And this is the spirit of the Antichrist, which you have heard was coming, and is now already in the world.* (1 John 4:3)

From time to time, as I have seen a person under a power of evil or having a fit, I have said to the power of evil or satanic force that is within the possessed person, "Did Jesus Christ come in the flesh?" and right away they have answered no. They either say no or hold their tongues, refusing altogether to acknowledge that the Lord Jesus Christ came in the flesh. It is at a time like this when, remembering that further statement of John's, *"He who is in you is greater than he who is in the world"* (1 John 4:4), you can, in the name of the Lord Jesus Christ, deal with the evil powers and command them to come out. We, as Pentecostal people, must know the tactics of the Evil One, and we must be able to displace and dislodge him from his position.

To discern spirits, we must dwell with Him who is holy, and He will give the revelation and unveil the mask of satanic power, whatever it is. In Australia, I went to one place where there were disrupted and broken homes. The people were so deluded by the evil power of Satan that men had left their wives and wives had left their husbands and they had gotten into spiritual affinity with one another. That is the Devil! May God deliver us from such evils in these days. There is no one better than the companion God has given you. I have seen so many broken hearts and so many homes that have been wrecked. We need a real revelation of these evil seducing spirits who come in and fascinate through the eyes, and who destroy lives, bringing the work of God into disrepute. But there is always flesh behind it. It is never clean; it is unholy, impure, satanic, devilish; and hell is behind it. If the Enemy comes in to tempt you in any way like this, I implore you to look instantly to the Lord Jesus.

He can deliver you from any such satanic power. You must be separated in every way if you are going to have faith.

The Holy Spirit will give us this gift of the discerning of spirits if we desire it so that we may perceive by revelation this evil power that comes in to destroy. We can reach out and get this unction of the Spirit that will reveal these things to us.

People will come to your meetings who are Spiritualists. You must be able to deal with spiritualistic conditions. You can deal with them in such a way that they will not have any power in the meetings. If you ever have mystics or Christian Scientists in your meetings, you must be able to discern them and deal with them. Never play with them; always clear them out. They are always better with their own company, unless they are willing to be delivered from the delusion they are in. Remember the warning of the Lord Jesus: *"The thief does not come except to steal, and to kill, and to destroy"* (John 10:10).

Seek the Lord, and He will sanctify every thought, every action, until your whole being is ablaze with holy purity and your one desire is for Him who has created you in holiness. Oh, this holiness! Can we be made pure? We can. Every inbred sin must go. God can cleanse away every evil thought. Can we have a hatred for sin and a love for righteousness? Yes, God will create within you a pure heart. He will take away your stony heart and give you a heart of flesh. He will sprinkle you with clean water, and you will be cleansed from all your filthiness (Ezek. 36:25–26). When will He do it? When you seek Him for such inward purity.

DELIVERANCE

Let me tell you what may seem to be a horrible story for you to hear; nevertheless, it is a situation in which discernment is necessary. This is happening all the time, and I do thank God for it because it is teaching me how to minister to people in the Lord.

Messages came to me again and again by telegraph, letters, and other things, asking that I come to London. I wired back and wrote, but so many calls came and no hint was given in any way as to the reason I was to go there. The only thing they said was that they were in great distress.

When I got there, the dear father and mother of the needy one both took me by the hand and broke down and wept.

"Surely this is deep sorrow of heart," I said.

They led me up onto the balcony. Then they pointed to a door that was open a little, and both of them left me. I went in that door and I have never seen a sight like it in all my life. I saw a young woman who was beautiful to look at, but she had four big men holding her down to the floor, and her clothing was torn from the struggle.

When I got into the room and looked into her eyes, her eyes rolled but she could not speak. She was exactly like the man in the Bible who came out of the tombs and ran to Jesus when he saw Him. As soon as he got to Jesus, he couldn't speak, but the demon powers spoke. (See Mark 5:1–13.) And the demon powers in this young girl spoke and said: "I know you. You can't cast us out; we are many."

"Yes," I said, "I know you are many, but my Lord Jesus will cast you all out."

It was a wonderful moment; it was a moment when it was only He alone who could do it.

The power of Satan was so great upon this beautiful girl that she whirled and broke away from these four strong men.

The Spirit of the Lord was wonderful in me, and I went right up to her and looked into her face. I saw the evil powers there; her very eyes flashed with demon power.

"In the name of Jesus," I said, "I command you to leave. Though you are many, I command you to leave this moment, in the name of Jesus."

She instantly became sick and began vomiting. She vomited out thirty-seven evil spirits and gave their names as they came out. That day she was made as perfect as anybody.

The next morning at ten o'clock, we all shared a meal together. Praise the Lord!

With the gift of discernment, you are in pursuit of divine thought; you are in pursuit of divine character; you are in pursuit of the deep, holy, inward intuition so that you might know what to do. The Lord of Hosts is in you, and the Lord of Hosts is with you; His desire is that you should know how you will be able to do it.

One time I was preaching in Doncaster, England, on the topic of faith, and a number of people were delivered. There was a man named Jack present who was greatly interested and moved by what he saw. He himself was suffering with a stiff knee and had yards and yards of flannel wound around it. After he got home, he said to his wife, "I have taken in Wigglesworth's message, and now I am going to act on it and get deliverance. Wife, I want you to be the audience."

He took hold of his knee and said, "Come out, you devil, in the name of Jesus." Then he said, "It is all right, wife." He took the yards and yards of flannel off and found he was all right without the bandage.

The next night he went to the little Primitive Methodist church where he worshipped. There were a lot of young people there who were in bad situations, and Jack had a tremendous ministry delivering his friends through the name of Jesus. He had been given to see that a great many ills to which flesh is heir are nothing else but the operation of the Enemy; but his faith had risen also, and he saw that in the name of Jesus there was a power that was more than a match for the Enemy.

I arrived one night at Gottenberg in Sweden and was asked to hold a meeting there. In the midst of the meeting, a man fell full length in the doorway. The evil spirit threw him down, manifesting itself and disturbing the whole meeting. I rushed to the door and laid hold of this man and cried out to the evil spirit within him, "Come out, you devil! In the name of Jesus, we cast you out as an evil spirit." I lifted him up and said, "Stand on your feet and walk in the name of Jesus." I don't know whether anybody in the meeting understood me except the interpreter, but the devils knew what I said. I spoke in English, but these demons in Sweden cleared out. A similar thing happened in Oslo, Norway.

The Devil will endeavor to fascinate people through the eyes and through the mind. One time a beautiful young woman was brought to me who had been fascinated with some preacher; just because he had not given her satisfaction on the lines of courtship and marriage, the Devil had taken advantage of the situation and had made her delirious and insane. They had brought her 250 miles in that condition. She had previously received the baptism in the Spirit.

You ask, "Is there any place for the Enemy in one who has been baptized in the Holy Spirit?" Our only safety is in going on with God and in constantly being filled with the Holy Spirit. You must not forget Demas. He must have been baptized with the Holy Spirit, for he appears to have been one of Paul's right-hand workers, but the Enemy got him to the place where he loved this present world, and he fell away (2 Tim. 4:10).

When they brought this young woman to me, I discerned the evil power right away and immediately cast the thing out in the name of Jesus. It was a great joy to present her before all the people in her right mind again.

There is a life of perfect deliverance, and this is where God wants you to be. If I find that my peace is disturbed in any way, I know it is the Enemy who is trying to work. How do I know this? Because the Lord has promised to keep your mind in perfect peace when it is focused on Him (Isaiah 26:3). Paul told us to present our bodies as *"a living sacrifice, holy, acceptable to God, which is* [our] *reasonable service"* (Rom. 12:1). The Holy Spirit also spoke this word through Paul: *"And do not be conformed to this world, but be transformed by the renewing of your mind, that you may prove what is that good and acceptable and perfect will of God"* (v. 2).

Paul further told us in Philippians 4:8:

Finally, brethren, whatever things are true, whatever things are noble, whatever things are just, whatever things are pure, whatever

121

*things are lovely, whatever things are of good
report, if there is any virtue and if there is anything praiseworthy; meditate on these things.*
(Phil. 4:8)

As we think about what is pure, we become
pure. As we think about what is holy, we become
holy. And as we think about our Lord Jesus Christ,
we become like Him. We are changed into the likeness of the object on which our gaze is fixed.

HOW TO KNOW THE MIND OF GOD

Now we come to the place of how to know the
nature of the spirit we are dealing with. That is a
very important thing. You are always in a dangerous
place if you trust in your own knowledge. Let me say
to you that whatever the Holy Spirit does in these
days, He does in order to give you a new mind. Our
new mind is to have the thoughts of Christ, the mind
of Christ.

To have the thoughts and mind of Christ means
that you will never seek to assert yourself for your
own glory; now Another who is greater than you has
to take your place and lead you to where you are in
the place of Jesus. And in that way, the Lord will
give you power to discern evil spirits.

We have struck one of the most holy chords that
could be struck. I have clear confidence that we are
in the will of God in this meeting, and I know the
Lord is helping me to speak to you.

HINDRANCES TO DISCERNMENT

I want you to see clearly that you will never be
able to discern or deal with evil powers as long as

there is anything in you that the Devil can touch. You are only able to do what God desires for you to do as you have come into the depths of death to self, so that the supernatural life of Christ is abounding in you to destroy the powers of evil.

Before Satan can bring his evil spirits, there has to be an open door. Hear what the Scriptures say: *"The wicked one does not touch him"* (1 John 5:18), and *"The LORD shall preserve you from all evil; He shall preserve your soul"* (Ps. 121:7). How does Satan get an opening? When the believer ceases to seek holiness, purity, righteousness, truth; when he ceases to pray, stops reading the Word, and gives way to carnal appetites. Then it is that Satan comes. So often sickness comes as a result of disobedience. David said, *"Before I was afflicted I went astray"* (Ps. 119:67).

You will never be able to reach out your hand to destroy the power of Satan as long as there is the vestige of human desire or attainment in you. It is in the death of the death that you are in the life of the life. Don't fool yourself; don't mislead yourself. Never think that God overlooks sins. Sins have to be dealt with, and the only way God ever deals with sin is to absolutely destroy its power. You can be made so clean that the Devil comes and finds nothing in you. (See John 14:30.) And then you have power by the power of God over the powers of Satan.

Discernment is not mind or eye. Discernment is an intuition. Your heart knows exactly what you are dealing with, and you are dealing with it because of your heart purity against evil and uncleanness.

God is purifying me in every meeting. I can safely say that unless the power of the Spirit purges me through and through, I cannot help you. First of all, before I can give any life to you, the life must be in me. And remember that the Scriptures are very clear: death works in us so that life may work in you. (See 2 Corinthians 4:12.)

Now, the death that is working is all carnal, evil, sensual. Don't forget the remarkable thing in the Scriptures that leads us to this; there are sixty-six evil things listed in the Bible, such as murder, covetousness, evil propensities. But I am here to say by the power of God that one fruit will destroy every evil thing. *"Seek first the kingdom of God and His righteousness, and all these things shall be added to you"* (Matt. 6:33).

ELEVEN

How to Discern Voices

here are many voices in the world. I want you to be able to understand voices, to understand spiritual voices, to understand exactly what the Scripture means about these things.

Now, I know there are a good many people who are big on the author Sir Arthur Conan Doyle, who, you will find, is trying to delve into mysteries. There is nothing mystical about what we are doing, and I want to tell everybody who comes to this place that you will have no share with us if you have anything to do with spiritualism. We denounce it as being of the Devil, and we don't want fellowship with you. If you want to join up with two things—the Lord and the Devil—the Devil will get you in the end.

Now, what is the difference between the spirit of *"disobedience"* (Eph. 2:2) and the spirit of *"lawlessness"* (2 Thess. 2:7–8)? They are one and the same. They are the spirit of antichrist, and they are right in the midst of things. Spiritualism, Jehovah's Witnesses, Christian Science—they are all related. They have no room for the blood of Jesus, and you cannot get near God except by the blood; it is impossible. The blood is the only power that can make a clear road into the kingdom for you—the blood of Jesus.

TESTING THE SPIRITS

> *Beloved, do not believe every spirit, but test the spirits, whether they are of God; because many false prophets have gone out into the world. By this you know the Spirit of God: Every spirit that confesses that Jesus Christ has come in the flesh is of God, and every spirit that does not confess that Jesus Christ has come in the flesh is not of God. And this is the spirit of the Antichrist, which you have heard was coming, and is now already in the world. You are of God, little children, and have overcome them, because He who is in you is greater than he who is in the world. They are of the world. Therefore they speak as of the world, and the world hears them. We are of God. He who knows God hears us; he who is not of God does not hear us. By this we know the spirit of truth and the spirit of error.* (1 John 4:1–6)

Beloved, you have to be in a position to try the spirits to see whether they are of God. Why should believers try the spirits? You can always try the spirits to see whether they are of God for this reason: you will be able to tell the true revelation, and the true revelation that will come to you will always sanctify the heart; it will never have an "if" in it. When the Devil came to Jesus, he had an "if." He said, *"If You are the Son of God"* (Matt. 4:3), and *"If*

You will fall down and worship me" (v. 9). The Holy Spirit never comes with an "if." The Holy Spirit is the divine Orator of this wonderful Word, but the position of the mystic Conan Doyle, and others like him, is satanic.

I have often dealt with people under evil powers, people in fits and other things, and sometimes I have come across people so much controlled by evil powers that every time they want to speak, the evil powers speak. It is a very dangerous condition; but, it is true, people get possessed by the Devil.

Do you remember the biblical account of the man in the tomb who was terribly afflicted with evil powers (Mark 5:2–15)? Strong cords and chains could not hold him. Night and day, there he was in the tombs, *"crying out and cutting himself with stones"* (v. 5). Jesus came on the scene, and these evil powers caused the man to run. Now, it was all in the power of the Devil, and as soon as the man got in front of Jesus, the evil spirit said, *"Have You come here to torment us before the time?"* (Matt. 8:29). This man had no power to get free, but these evil spirits were so troubled in the presence of Jesus that they cried out, *"Have You come here to torment us before the time?"*

Oh, thank God for Jesus. I want you to notice that Jesus wants you to be so under His power, so controlled by and filled with the Holy Spirit, that the power of authority in you will resent all evil.

This is an important lesson for believers, because there are so many believers who are not on their guard. I want to impress you with the fact that every believer should reach a place in the Holy Spirit where he has no desire except the desire of God. The

Holy Spirit has to possess us until we are filled, led, yes, divinely led, by the Holy Spirit. It is a mighty thing to be filled with the Holy Spirit.

INTERPRETATION OF TONGUES

The Lord, He is the mighty power of government, for the Scripture says, "The government shall be upon His shoulders," and now He has taken us on His shoulders; therefore, let Him lead you where He will.

Do not desire to lead Jesus; if He leads you, He will lead you into truth. He will lead you into nothingness, but when you are in nothingness, you will be in power. He will lead you into weakness, but when you are in weakness, God will be with you in might; everything that seems weak from a human perspective will be under the control of divine power.

RECEIVING IMPRESSIONS

Now I want to deal with a very important thing. I have people by the hundreds who are continually pressing on me with their difficulties, with their strange and yet holy and noble desires, where two ways meet and they do not know which one to take. Some have received impressions in their minds and hearts, but I want to show you what comes of impressions.

A person came to me one day and said, "Oh, you know the Spirit of the Lord was mighty upon me this morning."

I said, "Good!"

"Oh, I want to tell you about it. I want you to tell me if there is such a place as Ingerow anywhere near here."

I answered, "Yes, there is."

"Well, that place has been on my mind; I have to go and preach there."

There was nothing wrong with his desire to go preach, was there?

But I asked, "What is the message?"

"I don't exactly know."

"Now come, what is the message?" I asked.

"Oh, I have to speak to someone about his soul."

"And you don't know that there is such a place? The place is toward Skipton," I replied.

"But I have to go."

"Now come," I said, "I want you to think. You are working, are you not? Do you think anybody in the mill will approve of you going to a place you don't know, to speak to someone you don't know?"

Was it of God? That is the first thing. It was an impression, coming from a desire to be something special. That's the danger. My daughter tried to stop her, but she went the first chance she got. She got to the station, and there was nobody there. The result was that she was soon in an asylum.

What was it? An impression. How will we know when this is the case?

A lady came to me yesterday and said, "Don't you know, the Spirit of the Lord is upon me; I have to preach the Gospel."

I said, "There is nothing wrong in that."

"I want to know where I have to go to preach, so I have come to you to see if the Lord has told you where I am to go."

"Yes, you have to begin at home. Begin at Jerusalem, and if you are successful, go to Judea; then if you are successful, God will send you to the uttermost parts of the world."

God is not going to send you to the uttermost parts of the world until you have been successful around Jerusalem. We have a tremendously big job; it is well worth doing, and I want to do it well. I want to tell you the difference between the right and the wrong way to discern voices and thoughts that may come into your minds.

You have the Scriptures, and you have the Holy Spirit. The Holy Spirit has wisdom, and He does not expect you to be foolish. The Holy Spirit has perfect insight into knowledge and wisdom, and truth always gives you balance.

You always need to have one thing removed from you: being terribly afraid. However, fear leaves, and power and confidence come in its place. You also need to have another thing that must remain, and that is love: love in order to obey God rather than your inclinations to be something; but if God wants to make you someone, that is different.

My wife tried her best to make me someone, but she could not do it. Her heart was right; her love was right; she did her best to make me a preacher. She used to say, "Now, Father, you could do it if you wanted to, and I want you to preach next Sunday."

I did everything to get ready; I tried everything. I don't know what I did not try—it would be best not to tell you what I did try. I had as many notes as would suit a clergyman for a week.

My wife's heart, her love, her desires were all right, but when I got up to preach, I would give out my text and then say, "If anybody can preach, now is your chance, for I have finished." That did not take place once, but many times. She was determined, and I was willing. When I ministered to those who had come forward to repent and receive Jesus, I could bring them right into the kingdom. I could nurse the children while my wife preached, and I was pleased to do it. But, don't you know, when the Holy Spirit came, then I was ready. Then the preaching abilities were not mine but the Lord's. To be filled with the Holy Spirit is to be filled with divine equipping. It must all be for Jesus.

Oh, I tell you, whatever you may think about it, the whole thing is that there is nothing good without Jesus. Anyone could jump on this platform and say, "I am right." But when you have no confidence, then Jesus is all the confidence you require. God must have men and women on fire for Him. God will mightily send you forth in the anointing of the Spirit, and sinners will feel convicted, but it will never be accomplished if you have it in your mind that you are going to be something. The baptism is a baptism of death, and you live only unto God.

The Holy Spirit versus Deceptive Voices

A lot of people are very much troubled by voices. Some people are so troubled that they get very distressed. Some people take it as a great thing; they think it is very remarkable, and they go astray. Lots of people go astray by foolish prophecy, and lots of people are foolish enough to believe that they have tongues and interpretation and that they can be told what they should do. This is altogether outside the plan of God and bordering on blasphemy.

I do not preach my own ideas. That is, I never come on this platform and tell you what I think, because everybody can think. I come on this platform to tell you what I know. Therefore, what you need to do is to listen to what I know so that you may learn it. Then you can tell others what you have learned so that they will learn also.

How can I dislodge the power of Satan? How can I deal with satanic power? How may I know whether a voice is of God or not? Are there not voices that come from God? Yes. I am here believing that I am in the right place to build you on the authority of the Word of God. I believe I am in the right place to build you so that you will be able to deal with the things that I am talking about. I have come with a knowledge of how to deal with these things, because I myself have been dealing with them.

> *By this you know the Spirit of God: Every spirit that confesses that Jesus Christ has come in the flesh is of God, and every spirit that does not confess that Jesus Christ has come in the flesh is not of God.* (1 John 4:2–3)

> *The grace of the Lord Jesus Christ, and the love of God, and the communion of the Holy Spirit be with you all.* (2 Cor. 13:14)

The first Scripture tells us how to deal with power that is not of God but is satanic. The second Scripture reveals that we have within us a secure position in God so that we may have the communion of the Holy Spirit, who has all the latest plans, thoughts, and language from heaven. You know that a business executive is one who has a right to declare everything for the board of directors. And the Chief Executive of the world is the Holy Spirit. He is here today as a communication to our hearts, to our minds, to our thoughts, of what God wants us to know. So this Holy Executive, who is in us, can speak wonderful words. In fact, you will find that the Holy Executive will speak most of the words in this sermon.

I am dealing now with what you may know when you are fully in the Holy Spirit. The Spirit will teach you; He will *"bring to your remembrance all things"* (John 14:26). Now you do not need any man to teach you. But the anointing remains (1 John 2:27). You do not need teachers, but you need the Teacher, who is the Holy Spirit, to bring all things to your remembrance. This is the office of the Holy Spirit. This is the power of His communication. This is what John meant when he said, *"God is love"* (1 John 4:8). Jesus, who is grace, is with you. But the Holy Spirit is the speaker, and He speaks everything concerning Jesus.

There may be people here who have been hearing voices, and it has put them in a situation in which they have been moving from place to place. I am referring to voices that have caused tremendous issues in your lives, brought a great amount of distress and brokenheartedness, and led you into confusion and trouble. Why? You did not know how to judge the voices.

If a voice comes and tells you what to do, if a person comes and says he has a special prophecy

that God has given him for you, you have as much
right to ask God for that prophecy as they had to
give it to you, and you have as much right to judge
that prophecy according to the Word of God. You
need to do this, for there are people going about pre-
tending to be tremendous people, and they are
sending people nearly off their wits' end because
they believe their damnable prophecies, which never
are of God but are of the Devil. I am very severe on
this thing. God won't let me rest; I have to deal with
these things because I find people everywhere in a
terrible state because of these voices. How will we
get to know the difference between the voice of God
and the voice of Satan? The Scripture tells us.

INTERPRETATION OF TONGUES

God brings liberty and fruit, precious fruit,
holy fruit, inward piety, holiness, entirety,
separatedness from the world, chastened by
the Lord, filled with light, admiration of Jesus, and you see Him above all, full of light
and truth, bringing forth into your hearts perfect peace and joy. This is tranquillity; this is
God's desire for you, every one of you, to be
filled with the joy of the Lord.

THE SPIRIT GIVES JOY AND GLADNESS

The difference between those who are being led
by the Holy Spirit and those who are being deceived
by Satan is joy, gladness, and a good countenance
instead of sadness, sorrow, and depression. When
Jesus comes with joy into the soul and lifts you
higher and higher, it is the Spirit who gives light.

When satanic power begins to rule, then there is weariness, then people's faces are like a tragedy, then their eyes glare as though they had passed through a terrible trial.

You are always right to *"test the spirits, whether they are of God"* (1 John 4:1). If you do not do it, then you will be sure to be caught napping.

MISLED BY A "VOICE"

I want to describe some specific cases to further explain this. Two sisters were saved in our meetings and were filled with the Holy Spirit. They were very lovely women, full of purity, truth, and righteousness. Their expressions were good; no one could look at them without admiring them.

Both of them worked in a telegraph office, and they both desired to be missionaries. They were so zealous to be missionaries that they were laying aside money and everything they could in order to be prepared to go to the mission field. They were zealous for God. Their very lives would reveal this in a meeting or anywhere else. They were so zealous for God that they would do anything.

One of them was operating a telegraph machine when she heard a voice in her head, a voice that said something along these lines: "Will you obey me? If you will obey me, I will make you the most wonderful missionary that ever lived." Oh, beloved, try the voices, try the spirits. Only the Devil promises such a thing, but she did not know this; she did not understand. This was exactly what she wanted; it was her heart's desire, do you see? And she was so moved by this. The voice added, "And I will find you all the money you need."

I never knew this kind of "leading" to come true, and you never will as long as you live.

For example, a man came to me and said, "I have in my hands a certain food for invalids that can raise millions of dollars for the missionaries."

I said to him, "I will not have anything to do with it." These things are not a success. God does not work that way. If God wanted you to have gold, He could make it rain on your houses while you were away. He has all the gold, and the cattle on a thousand hills are His (Ps. 50:10).

Beloved, I want you to see that Jesus was the meekest man in the world. He had power to make bread or gold, and yet He never made it except for somebody else.

When anybody preaches for the kingdom's sake, God will provide. Seek to be filled with the Holy Spirit for the people's sake. Seek only God, and the rain will fall. The enduement of power will be made manifest in your mortal bodies if you are really in the Spirit.

Now, this young woman was so excited that her sister noticed it and went to her.

"What is it?" she asked.

"Oh! God is speaking to me," she said, "saying wonderful things to me."

She became so excited that her sister asked their supervisor if they could be excused for a while, because she saw that she would have to protect her. So the overseer allowed them both to be excused for a time, and they went into a room. The first sister became so excited with these messages, so believing that it was of God, that her white blouse became spotted with blood as she pricked her flesh with the nails of her hand.

That is never of God. What do I read about the wisdom of God? I read that it is full of peace and gentleness; it is willing to submit; it is without partiality; it is full of goodness and truth. (See James 3:17.) And, remember, if you ever know anything about God, it will be peace. If you ever know anything about the world, it will be disorder. The peace of God, which passes all understanding (Phil. 4:7), comes to the heart after you are saved. We are *"justified by faith,"* and *"we have peace with God through our Lord Jesus Christ"* (Rom. 5:1). The peace continues until it makes us full of the *"hope of the glory of God"* (v. 2).

God showed me a long time ago, and it has not been taken out of my mind, that if I was disturbed in my spirit and was not at rest, I had missed the plan. How can you miss it? In three ways.

First of all, you can miss it because you have taken on someone else's burden. All the time you are told to cast your burden on the Lord (1 Pet. 5:7). Any number of people are overflowing with sorrow because they are taking on someone else's burden. That is wrong. You must teach them and teach yourself that you have to cast your burdens on the Lord.

Secondly, if you do not have peace, you have gotten out of the will of God in some way. You may not have sinned. You can be out of the will of God without sinning. You can be out of the will of God if you are not making progress. If you have not made progress since yesterday morning, you are a backslider. Everybody is a backslider who is not going on with God. You are a backslider if you do not increase in the divine character and likeness of Christ. You have to move from state to state, *"from glory to glory"* (2 Cor. 3:18), by the Spirit of the Lord.

INTERPRETATION OF TONGUES

The Spirit quickens, moves, chastens, builds, builds, builds, and makes you free.

> This is like heaven to me,
> This is like heaven to me;
> I've crossed over Jordan to
>   Canaan's fair land
> And this is like heaven to me.

You won't be down in the dumps then. Do you know what Jordan represents? Jordan represents death, and you have crossed over death. Do not drop into it again.

You can lose your peace by missing some divine plan of God, and you can lose your peace because you have gotten your mind on something natural. A natural thing is a carnal thing. The Word of God says that the carnal things have to be destroyed because they are not subject to the law of God and cannot be subject to them (Rom. 8:7). Every carnal thing must be destroyed.

So you can miss the plan. Now, what is the plan? *"You will keep him in perfect peace, whose mind is stayed on You, because he trusts in You"* (Isa. 26:3). Examine yourself to see where you are. If you are not in perfect peace, you are out of the will of God.

Therefore, if these voices take away your peace, you will know they are not the will of God. But if the Spirit speaks, He will bring harmony and joy. The Spirit always brings three things: comfort, exhortation, and edification. He will make you sing *"songs in the night"* (Job 35:10). You will rise in high places, and you will not be afraid of declaring the works of the Lord. When the Spirit of the Lord is upon you and greatly active, you may *"go from strength to strength"* (Ps. 84:7), praising the Lord.

My wife and I were visiting at the home of these two sisters when they came in from work that day. We saw the distress. We saw the wild condition. If you are wild, that is the Devil. If you go breathlessly to the Bible, looking for confirmation of the voice, that is the Devil. The Word of God brings light. I must use it as the Word of Light. I must see it as the Light of Light. I must have it as the Light. I must not run up and down as if I had been hit with a stick.

I must be wise, because if I say I am baptized with the Holy Spirit, if I say I am a child of God, I must act so that people will know that I have been with God. (See Acts 4:13.) If there is anything I would resound through this meeting like a trumpet, it is this: *"Do not let your good be spoken of as evil"* (Rom. 14:16)!

Who is speaking now? It is the Spirit speaking to us, saying that He wants us in the world in such a way that we would not have anything—neither tongues, interpretations, prophecy, discernment, nor any kind of actions—except what would affirm that we have been with Jesus and that now the light has come, the truth has fallen upon us, and we have come into the wisdom of the Most High God. If you ever find a person who has given a prophecy but who will not allow that prophecy to be judged, as sure as anything, that prophecy never was right. Everybody who has a true prophecy is willing to come to the light so that everything will be made true according to the Word of God. So don't receive these things unless you know they are of God.

Well, what happened to the young woman? The voice came with such tremendous force that she could not let it go. Try the spirits. God will never do anything like that. He will never send you an unreasonable, unmanageable message.

The moment the girl became obsessed with what the voice said, what did the Devil say next? "You keep this a secret. Don't tell anybody. If you confide in anybody, let it be your sister, because she seems to understand you." So they confided in each other.

Now that is surely as satanic as anything you ever heard in your life, because every true thing, every holy thing, does not need to be kept a secret under any circumstances. Anything that is holy can be told on the housetops; God wants you to be able to tell all.

My wife and I tried to help them. "Oh, God is speaking to me!" the young woman said. And we could not change her. That night she said that the evil power continued speaking, saying to her, "Tell no one but your sister. Go to the station tonight and wait for the train. The train will come in at thirty-two minutes past seven. Buy two tickets for Glasgow. After you have bought your tickets, you will have sixpence left."

This could be confirmed, and no one had to know but her sister. They went to the station. The train came in exactly at the right time. And there was just sixpence left after they had bought the ticket. Marvelous! Wonderful! This was sure to be right.

"See!" she said. "I have just the amount of money left after I have bought the tickets that the voice said I would." The train came in. The voice had said that a gentleman would be sitting in one of the coaches with all the money she would ever need. Directly opposite this gentleman, a woman with a nurse's cap would be sitting. The man would give her all the money, and they were to take it to a certain bank at a certain street corner in Glasgow.

Here was lack of presentation of thought. There are no banks open at half past seven, and, after investigation, it was discovered that there was no such bank in that place. Then what caused the young woman to obey the voice? It got her ear, and I will tell you what the danger is. If I had only five minutes I would say this to you: If you cannot be reasoned with, you are wrong. If you are right and everybody else is wrong, I don't care who you are, if you cannot bear examination, if what you hold cannot bear the light of the truth, you are wrong. It will save a lot of you if you will just think.

You may say, "Oh, but I know, I *know*." It is a very serious thing when nobody else knows but you. May God deliver us from such a condition. If you think you have some specialty, it is not unique; it can be repeated.

The train came in. They rushed from one end of the train to the other. There were no such people on the train. Then the voice came, "On the next platform, the next train." And they rushed over. Would you believe, those two young women were kept moving from platform to platform by those voices until half past nine at night?

Those voices went on. Ah, those evil voices. How will we know whether they are of God? When God speaks, He will speak with wisdom. When the Devil came to Jesus he said, *"If You are the Son of God"* (Matt. 4:3). The Devil knew that He was the Son of God, and Jesus knew and answered, *"It is written, 'You shall worship the LORD your God, and Him only you shall serve'"* (v. 10).

Now, was there anything wrong with what was happening with these two young women? The wrong was that the first young woman ought to have judged the spirits. If she had asked, "Did Jesus come in the flesh?" the voice would have answered no. No satanic voice in the world and no Spiritualist medium will acknowledge that Jesus came in the flesh. The Devil never will, and he is the father of spiritualism mediums.

The same power said to the young woman, "Now that I know you will obey me in everything, I will make you the greatest missionary in the world."

We tried to console them, but nothing could be done; she was convinced it was the voice of the Lord.

There are two workings; the workings of the Spirit are always contrary to the workings of the flesh.

How could the two women have known at that moment that this was a false voice? Why, they could have known according to the Word of God. What does it say? *"Many false prophets have gone out into the world"* (1 John 4:1). Many, many voices, the Scripture says. Who are these false prophets after? Perhaps those with sincerity, earnestness, zeal, and purity. Who knows? These evil powers know. What is necessary to keep in our minds all the time? We must keep these things clearly in mind: What am I living for? What is the hope of my life? Do I have to be the greatest missionary in the world and a wonderful Christian worker, or does Jesus need to be glorified in my life to do as He wills with me for the world? The ripe grape is never as pure and perfect as it is just before it decays. The child of God is never as near to God—right at the summit—as he is when the Devil can come and say, "You are wonderful!"

It is satanic to feel that you are different from anybody else, that God has a special message for you, and that you are someone very particular. Every place that God brings you to in a rising tide of perfection is a place of humility, brokenness of heart, and fullness of surrender, where only God can rule in authority. It is not where you are somebody, but where God is everything and where you will be living for the exhibition of His glory.

It was three months before these two young women were delivered from this delusion. It took months and months of pleading, of crying bitterly. But God did deliver them, and they have been really wonderful missionaries in China. Thank God, there is a way out. The Devil's plan was defeated, but it was at tremendous cost, almost of their lives.

How could they have known that it was a false voice? How can you know? When a voice comes, no matter how it seems to you, you must test it. When a voice comes and it is strange, when it is persistently pressing you to do something and you are taken to a hard place and you know the difficulties are such that you can hardly conceive how this thing is possible, you have a position in the power of the Word of God to say to this evil power, "Did Jesus come in the flesh?" (1 John 4:3). And the satanic power will say no. There never yet was a Spiritualist or anybody else who was under satanic power, anybody in a fit, anybody losing his mind, who has ever said that Jesus came in the flesh. Satanic forces will not admit it.

But the Spirit of the living God, the Holy Spirit, always says yes. And so you can get to know the difference. You have to listen. The Scriptures are clear on these things. We have to live in the place of knowing so that we are able to spiritually, divinely discern whether these things are of God or not.

Did Jesus come in the flesh? Yes, and now the living Christ is within you. Christ came into you the moment you believed. There is a manifestation of it. You may live in such a way that Christ is greater than you. You may live in such a way that your language, your expressions, your actions, and everything speak of Christ. *"They realized that they had been with Jesus"* (Acts 4:13). You can live in such a way that the personality of Christ is exactly what Paul said: "Not I—I don't live anymore. Christ lives in me." (See Galatians 2:20.)

The Christ life, the Christ power, the personality of His presence may be in you in such a way that you could not doubt the Word of God. If you prayed, it would always be in faith, and as you preached, it would always be in faith. You *"live by the faith of the Son of God"* (Gal. 2:20 KJV) until your whole body is aflame with the faith of God. This is a divine position of a living attitude in which we live and reign in this beautiful place with Jesus.

This is an important word, and I am saying everything I can, by the grace of God and the revelation of the Spirit, to make you careful and yet careless: careful of satanic powers and careless when the power of God is upon you with anointing force, so that He Himself will be manifested, and not you.

A RUINED LIFE

Lots of people are brought down by the same thing that ruined the life of a young Christian I want to tell you about. For many years after I was baptized, the Lord graciously helped me. I laid hands upon people, and they received the Holy Spirit. I thank God that that power has not stopped. I believe in asking God, in lifting up holy hands and saying, "Father, grant that whoever I place my hands upon will receive the Holy Spirit."

People have called me from various places to come and help them when they have had people they wanted to receive the Holy Spirit. Once a group from York, England, sent word saying that they had fourteen people whom they wanted to have baptized in the Holy Spirit, and would I come? They had all been saved since the last time I was there.

So I went. I have never in all my life met a group of people who were so intoxicated with a certain thing, which had happened since I had been there. In the open-air preaching, the power of God had been upon them, and many people had been gathered from the marketplace. Right there in the midst of them, they had drawn in a young man who had developed such a gift of teaching and such a gift of leading the people forward with God through the power of the Spirit that they said they did not believe there was another man like him in all of England. They were intoxicated beyond anything; they were drunk with it.

Did I rejoice with them? Certainly.

If there is anything that I love, it is the young men and young women. When Jesus began His ministry, He laid hands upon eleven who turned out to be the most marvelous men, and yet they were all younger then He. When Paul was brought into the knowledge of the truth, he was a young man. Jesus began the great ministry of worldwide revival with young life.

World War I showed us that no man over forty years of age was good enough for that war. They had to have young blood, young life that could stand the stress of frost, heat, and all kinds of things.

God wants young people filled with the power of God to go into the harvest field, because they can stand the stress. Jesus knew this, and He got all young men around Him.

Weren't the disciples a lovely group? Yes, when He was in the midst of them. You are a lovely group of people because Jesus is in the midst of you, and you will be more lovely as you keep Him in your midst. You will be more lovely still if you refuse to live unless He is in your midst.

Moses said, *"If Your Presence does not go with us, do not bring us up from here"* (Exod. 33:15). And we have a right today to live in the presence of the power of the Holy Spirit.

As soon as I got to York, the people came around me and said, "Oh, we've got him! We've got him! The only thing that is needed now is that we want him to receive the Holy Spirit, and as soon as he receives, we will know we have got him."

Was anything wrong with that? No, I rejoiced with them.

Then the power of God fell. You know, we allow anything in a meeting before people receive the Spirit. Don't be afraid when people are on the floor. Lots of people roll around the floor and get their

146

black clothes made white. Any number of things take place when the flesh is giving way to the Spirit. But after the Holy Spirit has come in, then we do not expect you to roll again on the floor. We only expect you to roll on the floor until the life of the personality of the Holy Spirit has gotten right in and turned you out; then you will be able to stand up and preach instead of rolling on the floor.

The new believers were all lying on the floor. It was a wonderful sight. The people came to me and said, "Oh! Oh! We've got him now!" Oh, it was so lovely! And when that young man spoke in tongues, they almost went wild. They shouted, they wept, they prayed. Oh, they were so excited!

The leaders came and said they were overjoyed at the fact. I said, "Be still; the Lord will do His own work."

In a short time, he was through in the Spirit, and everybody was rejoicing and applauding. They fell into great error there.

Oh, I do pray that God will save you from anything like this. I hope nobody would say to me, "Oh, you did preach well tonight." It's as surely of the Devil as anything that ever came to anybody. God has never yet allowed any human being to be applauded.

This young man was in the power of the Holy Spirit, and it was lovely. But they came around him, shaking his hand and saying, "Now we have the greatest teacher there is."

Was this wrong? It was perfectly right, and yet it was the worst thing they could have done; they should have been thankful in their hearts. I want to tell you that the Devil never knows your thoughts, and if you won't let your thoughts out in public, you will be safe. He can suggest a thought; he can suggest thoughts of evil. But that is not sin; all these things are from outside of you. The Devil can suggest evil things for you to receive, but if you are pure, it is like water off a duck's back.

One woman came up and said, "I wouldn't be surprised if you had another John the Baptist."

And they were all around him, shaking hands and saying, "Oh, now we've got him! Now we know you are the best teacher that has ever been in Pentecost yet."

Thank God, the young man was able to throw it all off, and he was in a beautiful place.

Again, before we left, this woman came up and said, "Will you believe? It is a prophecy I have received that you have to be John the Baptist."

Thank God, he put it off again. But how satantic, how devilish, how unrighteous, and how untrue it was!

That night, as he was walking home along a country road, another voice came, louder than the woman's, right in the open air: "You are John the Baptist!"

Again the young man was able to guard it off. In the middle of the night, he was awakened out of his sleep, and this voice came again: "Rise, get up. You are John the Baptist. Declare it!"

And the poor man this time was not able to deal with it. He did not know what I am now telling you. I tell you with a sorrowful heart that for hours that morning he was walking around York, shouting, "I am John the Baptist!" Nothing could be done. He had to be detained.

Who did it? Why, the people, of course.

You have no right to come around me or anybody else and say, "You are wonderful!" That is satanic. I tell you, we have plenty of the Devil to deal with without your causing a thousand demons to come and help. We need common sense.

How could that young man have been delivered? He could have said, "Did Jesus come in the flesh?" The demon power would have said no, and then the Comforter would have come.

Lord, bring us to a place of humility and brokenheartedness where we will see the danger of satanic powers.

Don't think that the Devil is a big ugly monster; he comes as an angel of light (2 Cor. 11:14). He comes at a time when you have done well, and he tells you about it. He comes to make you feel you are somebody. The Devil is an exalted demon.

Oh, look at the Master. If you could see Him as I see Him sometimes: He was rich, and yet He became poor (2 Cor. 8:9); He was in the glory, yet He took upon Himself the form of a servant (Phil. 2:6–7). Yes, a servant, that is the Lord. May God give us the mindset of the Beatitudes (Matt. 5:3–12) where we will be broken and humble and in the dust; then God will raise us and place us in a high place.

These are days when God wants you to build. God does not want to take away your glory; He wants you to have the glory, for Jesus came and said, *"And the glory which You gave Me I have given them"* (John 17:22). But what is the glory for? To place on the Master. Give Him all; let Him have all: your heart's joy, your very life. Let Him have it. He is worthy. He is King of Kings. He is Lord of Lords. He is my Savior. He died to deliver me. He should have the crown.

TWELVE

TESTING THE SPIRITS

od has never changed His mind concerning His promises. They are *"Yes"* and *"Amen"* (2 Cor. 1:20) to those who believe. God is the same yesterday and forever (Heb. 13:8). To doubt Him is sin. All unbelief is sin. So we have to believe He can heal, save, fill with the Holy Spirit, and transform us altogether.

Are you ready? What for? To be so chastened by the Lord, so corrected by Him that, as you pass through the fire, as you pass through all temptations, you may come out as Jesus came out of the wilderness, filled with the Spirit.

Are you ready? What for? To be so brought in touch with the Father's will that you may know that whatever you ask, believing, you will receive (Matt. 21:22). This is the promise; this is the reality God brings to us.

Are you ready? What for? To no longer know yourself according to the flesh, to no longer yield to the flesh, but to be quickened by the Spirit, living in the Spirit without condemnation, your testimony bright, cheerful, and full of life. This is the inheritance for you today.

DO NOT BELIEVE EVERY SPIRIT

The message the Lord wants me to speak to you about is in the fourth chapter of 1 John. I would like the day to come in which we would never come to a meeting without having the Word of God with us. The great need today is to have more of the Word. There is no foundation apart from the Word. The Word not only gives you a foundation, but it also puts you in a place where you can stand and, after the battle, keep on standing. Nothing else will do it. When the Word is in your heart, it will preserve you from desiring sin. The Word is the living presence of that divine power that overcomes the world. You need the Word of God in your hearts so that you might be able to overcome the world.

> *Beloved, do not believe every spirit, but test the spirits, whether they are of God; because many false prophets have gone out into the world. By this you know the Spirit of God: Every spirit that confesses that Jesus Christ has come in the flesh is of God, and every spirit that does not confess that Jesus Christ has come in the flesh is not of God. And this is the spirit of the Antichrist, which you have heard was coming, and is now already in the world.*
>
> (1 John 4:1–3)

If this passage were honeycombed right through our own circumstances, there would be no room for fear. We are dealing with a subject concerning satanic power so that we may be able to discern evil spirits.

We can so live in this divine communion with Christ that we can sense evil in any part of the world. In this present world, powers of evil are rampant. The man who lives in God is afraid of nothing. The plan of God is that we might be so in Him that we will be equal to any occasion.

"Beloved" (1 John 4:1). That is a good word. It means that we are now in a place where God has set His love upon us. He wants us to listen to what He has to say to us because when His beloved are hearing His voice, then they understand what He has for them.

The passage continues:

You are of God, little children, and have overcome them, because He who is in you is greater than he who is in the world. They are of the world. Therefore they speak as of the world, and the world hears them. We are of God. He who knows God hears us; he who is not of God does not hear us. By this we know the spirit of truth and the spirit of error. Beloved, let us love one another, for love is of God; and everyone who loves is born of God and knows God. He who does not love does not know God, for God is love. In this the love of God was manifested toward us, that God has sent His only begotten Son into the world, that we might live through Him. In this is love, not that we loved God, but that He loved us and sent His Son to be the propitiation for our sins. Beloved, if God so loved us, we also ought to love one another. No one has seen God at any time. If we love one another, God abides in us, and His love has been perfected in us. By this we know that we abide in Him, and He in us, because He has given us of His Spirit. And we have seen and testify that the Father has sent the Son as Savior of the world. Whoever confesses that Jesus is the Son of God, God abides in him, and he in God. And we have known and believed the love that God has for us. God is love, and he who abides in love abides in God, and God in him. Love has been perfected among us in this: that we may have boldness in the day of judgment; because as He is, so are we in this world. There is no fear in love; but perfect love casts out fear, because fear involves torment. But he who fears has not been made perfect in love. We love Him because He first loved us.

(1 John 4:4–19)

This is an inexhaustible subject. We should get a great deal out of this message that will serve us for an evil day and the day of temptation.

God is dealing with us as sons; He calls us *"beloved."* We are in the truth, but we want to know the truth in a way that will keep us free. (See John 8:32.) I want to help the people who have been so troubled with voices and with things that have happened that they have felt they had no control over them. And I want to help those people who are bound in many ways and have been trying in every way to get free. I believe the Lord wants me very definitely to deal with things that will be of an important nature to you as long as you live.

The fourth chapter of 1 John tells us specifically how to deal with evil powers, with evil voices. It tells us how we may be able to dethrone them and be in a place where we are over them. It shows us how we may live in the world not subject to fear, not subject to bondage, not subject to pain, but in a place where we are defeating evil powers, ruling over them, reigning in the world by this life of Christ. In this way, we will be from above, and we will know it. We will not be subject to the world, but we will reign over the world so that disease, sin, and death will not have dominion.

A keynote that runs through the entire Scriptures is that Jesus has vanquished and overcome all of the powers of the Devil and has destroyed his power, even the power of death. Whether we are going to believe it or not, this is for us. God sends out the challenge, and He says, "If you believe it, it will be so."

What will hinder us? Our human nature will. This has a lot to do with hindering God: when the human will is not wholly surrendered, when there is some mixture, part spirit and part flesh, when there is a division in your own heart.

In a house where there are two children, one may desire to obey his father and mother, and he is loved and is very well treated. The other is loved just the same, but the difficulty is this: the wayward boy who wants his own way does many things to grieve his parents, and he gets the whip. They are both children in the house; one is getting the whip, the other is getting the blessing without the whip.

There are any number of God's children who are getting the whip who know better than they are doing. So I want you to wake up to do what you know ought to be done, because there is a whipping for those who won't obey. Sin is never covered by your appearance, your presence, your prayers, or your tears. Sin can only be removed by repentance. When you repent deeply enough, you will find that the thing goes away forever. Never cover up sin. Sins must be judged. Sins must be brought to the blood of Christ. When you have a perfect confidence between you and God, it is amazing how your prayers rise. You catch fire, you are filled with zeal, your inspiration is tremendous, you find out that the Spirit prays through you, and you live in a place of blessing.

DEALING WITH EVIL POWERS

There are many people living today who are called Spiritualists. I call them "Devilists." I never give any quarter to them. If I see a spiritualism meeting advertised, I say, "There is a Devil-possessed meeting." I never encounter a Christian Scientist without knowing he is also working the powers of darkness and that he is on the Devil's side. I never meet a Jehovah's Witness without knowing that he has changed the Word of God, and I know that God has removed him from the blessing.

INTERPRETATION OF TONGUES

On the housetop things will be declared. God will bring everything to light that has been in darkness. There is not one thing but what will have to be judged, and in the present time the believer in Christ is in the position of judging the Devil. The Prince of this World is judged, and God is fulfilling His divine power when He is bringing us into perfect order through the Spirit, so that we voice the power of the Word of God, so that we deal with satanic influences, satanic power.

In this world we are to overcome until we deal with every demon power, so that Christ comes at the top and reigns over us, because He has given us power and authority over all the power of the Devil.

So God, by the power of the Spirit, has given us a revelation of our position in Christ. Whatever happens in the world, we must see that every demon power must be dislodged, cast into the pit forever. We must recognize that God's Son is placed in power over the power of the Enemy; we must understand that anybody who deals falsely with the Word of God nullifies the position of authority that Christ has given him over Satan.

What did Christ say? In a very definite way, He said:

If your hand causes you to sin, cut it off. It is better for you to enter into life maimed, rather than having two hands, to go to hell, into the fire that shall never be quenched; where "their worm does not die, and the fire is not quenched." And if your foot causes you to sin, cut it off. It is better for you to enter life lame, rather than having two feet, to be cast into hell, into the fire that shall never be quenched; where "their worm does not die, and the fire is not quenched." And if your eye causes you to sin, pluck it out. It is better for you to enter the kingdom of God with one eye, rather than having two eyes, to be cast into hell fire; where "their worm does not die, and the fire is not quenched." (Mark 9:43–48)

It is better to go into the presence of God with half your faculties than to go into hell with all your faculties. Jesus knew that hell was a reality, and He gave no quarter to it. And when He was dealing with demons, they were referred to as *"unclean spirit*[s]*,"* (Mark 9:25 KJV), meaning that there is no clean demon power. All demon powers are unclean.

God wants a clean people. He is cleansing us from all the filthiness of the flesh so that when the Devil comes, he will find nothing in us. (See John 14:30.)

JUDGE YOURSELF BY GOD'S WORD

There are two ways of being in the place where God wants you to be. One is to see that you obey. The next is to examine yourself to see that *"you are in the faith"* (2 Cor. 13:5). If you do not judge yourself, you will be judged (1 Cor. 11:31). But if you judge yourself by the Word of God, you will not be condemned with the present evil world (v. 32).

SPIRITUALISTS REMOVED

One day we were having a meeting after the Holy Spirit came upon us, and the word got around that we had received the baptism of the Spirit, as we called it, and were speaking in tongues. Many people said we had received satanic power and were speaking in tongues through the power of the Devil. So the whole city was awakened. At this meeting there were two rows of Spiritualists—these demon-possessed people. The power of the Spirit was upon me, and I began speaking in tongues, and these demon powers began muttering, shaking, rolling, and all kinds of things.

I went off the platform, stood at the end of the two rows, and said, "Come out, you demons, in the name of Jesus!" The two rows of people filed out of their seats and went down the aisle and outside. When they got outside, they cursed and blasphemed and said all kinds of evil things. But thank God they were outside!

Mediums Hindered

One day I met a friend of mine in the street, and I said, "Fred, where are you going?"

"I am going—. Oh, I don't feel I ought to tell you," he said. "It is a secret between me and the Lord."

"Now, we have prayed together, we have had nights of communication, we have been living together in the Spirit," I said. "Surely there is no secret that could be hidden between you and me."

"I will tell you," he said. "I am going to a spiritualism meeting."

"Don't you think it is dangerous? I don't think it is wise for believers to go to these places," I said.

"I am led to go to test it according to Scripture," he replied. "They are having some special mediums from London."

He meant that they were having some people from London who were more filled with the Devil than the Spiritualists we had in our city of Bradford. They were special devils.

"I am going," he continued, "and I am going with the clear knowledge that I am under the blood of Jesus."

"Tell me the results, will you?"

"Yes, I will."

Now, beloved, I advise none of you to go to these places.

My friend went and sat down in the midst of the séance meeting, and the medium began to take control. The lights went low; everything was in a dismal state. My friend did not speak, but just kept himself under the blood, whispering the preciousness of the blood of Jesus. These more possessed devils were on the platform. They tried every possible thing they could to get under control for more than an hour, and then the lights went up. The leader said, "We can do nothing tonight; there is somebody here who believes in the blood of Christ."

Hallelujah! Do you all believe in the blood, beloved?

INTERPRETATION OF TONGUES

See that you keep your heart in a place where the blood is covering you, where the wicked one does not touch you, for has He not given "charge over you to keep you in all your ways"? He will send His angels, and "they will bear you up, lest you dash your foot against a stone." It is the Lord your God who overshadows; it is the Lord your God who protects, for He "will not slumber or sleep," but He keeps you in the perfect place, like "the apple of His eye," in perfection.

GREATER IS HE WHO IS IN YOU

"Test the spirits, whether they are of God" (1 John 4:1). Be ready to challenge the Devil. Don't be afraid. You will be delivered from fear if you believe.

You can have *"ears to hear"* (Matt. 11:15) or ears that do not hear. Ears that hear are the ears of faith, and your ears will be so open to what is spiritual that they will lay hold of it.

When the Word of God becomes the life and nature of you, you will find that the minute you open it, it becomes life to you; you will find that you have to be joined up with the Word. You are to be the epistles of Christ (2 Cor. 3:3). This means that Christ is the Word, and He will be known in us by our fruits. (See Matthew 7:16–20.) He is the life and the nature of you. It is a new nature: a new life, a new breath, a new spiritual atmosphere. There is no limitation in this standard, but in everything else you are limited. *"He who is in you is greater than he who is in the world"* (1 John 4:4). When the Word of Life is lived out in you because it is your life, then it is enacted, and it brings forth what God has desired. When we quote something from the Scriptures, we must be careful that we are living according to it. The Word of God has to abide in you, for the Word is life and it brings forth life, and this is the life that makes you *"free from the law of sin and death"* (Rom. 8:2).

HOW TO TEST THE SPIRITS

There are evil thoughts, and there are thoughts of evil. Evil thoughts are suggestive of the Evil One. We must be able to understand what the evil is and how to deal with it. The Word of God makes us strong. All evil powers are weak. There is nothing strong in the Devil; the weakest believer dethrones the Enemy when he mentions Jesus. "Young men, you are strong because you know the Word." (See 1 John 2:14.)

There are evil thoughts and thoughts of evil. Where do thoughts of evil come from? They come from the unclean believer, the man who is not entirely sanctified. Remember that the Devil does not know your thoughts; that is where the Devil is held. But God knows your thoughts; God knows all things. Satan can only suggest evil thoughts to try to arouse your carnal nature.

Yet if you are disturbed, if you are weak, if you are troubled or depressed, then you are in a wonderful place. If you never tell anybody about your evil thoughts, and you are not disturbed about them, the carnal powers have never been destroyed in you. But if you tell anybody, then it is proof that you are clean; it is because you are clean that you weep. If you are not disturbed, if you have no conviction, it is because of your uncleansed heart; you have let sin come in.

OVERCOMING EVIL POWERS

How can the believer believe so that he will not be tormented? The question is: How can we be master of the situation? We must know this Scripture: *"Every spirit that confesses that Jesus Christ has come in the flesh is of God"* (1 John 4:2). Did Jesus come in the flesh? Mary produced a Son in the likeness of God. In a similar way, the eternal seed that came into us when we believed produces a life, a person, which is *"Christ in* [us]*"* (Col. 1:27) and which rises up in us until the reflection of the Son of God is in everything we do. Mary produced a Son for redemption. God's seed in us produces a son of perfect redemption, until we live in Him and move by Him, and our whole nature becomes a perfect Son of God in us (Acts 17:28). In the name of Jesus, cast self out, and you will be instantly free.

The Holy Spirit has all power and all language. If you won't tell anybody when these suggestive evil powers come, it is proof that you are not sanctified. A Spiritualist will never say that Jesus came in the flesh. The Lord wants us to understand that spiritualistic evidences, and the like, are of the Devil.

A Place of Discernment

We must be in a place where we can discern evil things and evil spirits. There is a place where we can bind these evil powers and, loosing the people, set them free. Read the ninth chapter of Mark. There is an exchange of life, of power, until it is absolutely as the Word says: *"He who is in you is greater than he who is in the world"* (1 John 4:4). God can change you until you will not be afraid of anything.

Life comes after you have been filled with the Holy Spirit. Get down and pray for power. You ask, "What is the problem when I come away from prayer and nothing changes?" There are two reasons for this. First, when you go into your place, lock the door. Should you pray silently? No—pray loudly. The Devil has never disturbed anybody who prayed aloud. There the Holy Spirit's power is a proof.

Next, if you will, you can rebuke, you can cast out, satanic powers. Rebuke Satan. Never cast a demon out twice, or he will run about and laugh at you. He will know you did not believe it the first time. *"Ask, and you will receive"* (John 16:24). The moment you ask, believe you will receive, and you will have it.

Now I am going to pray, "Father, in the name of Jesus, increase my compassion." Thank You, Lord, I have it. I know I have it.

THIRTEEN

QUESTIONS AND ANSWERS ON TESTING SPIRITS

Q: Do you claim that there is no shaking of the body after the baptism of the Holy Spirit?

A: I maintain that after anyone has received the Holy Spirit, there is no shaking and no falling on the ground. Shaking and falling on the ground is a very limited position, instead of an unlimited position. There may be a manifestation, but it is not edifying, and the manifestation you are to have is to be for edification. (See 1 Corinthians 14:12.)

If somebody were to stand up now and shake and shake until her hair came down, no one in the place would be edified, and no one would want it. If the person knew it was not edifying, she would seek a place that is better. What is that better place? To seek a gift.

I declare to you that no one can shake and do all these things and speak in tongues. The Spirit has a way out. And no one when giving an interpretation has these manifestations, because the Holy Spirit has a way out. You need to seek so that you may excel and not be doing things that bring discord and discredit to your position.

Q: Is it true that tongues and interpretation are not for personal guidance at any time?

A: Tongues and interpretation are never for guidance. There is no such thing in the Scriptures. Tongues and interpretation are similar to prophecy; they are to edify the church.

Q: Can satanic influences come to us in thought as well as audibly, in word?

A: Any number of people are troubled with thoughts. There are two kinds of thoughts: evil thoughts and thoughts of evil. Evil thoughts are suggestive powers that the Devil gives to see if he can arouse your carnal nature. If he can, it shows you have never been changed from your corruption and sin. If he cannot, it shows you are pure; the blood has cleansed you, and carnality is defeated. This is what Jesus meant when He said that when the Devil comes, he finds nothing in you. (See John 14:30.)

The Devil does not know your thoughts; he does not know the desire of your hearts; he does not know your language. Therefore, the Devil always suggests something in order to get something from you. If we would only realize that fact, we could come into meetings and bind this power so that Satan would have no chance at all. Jesus said, *"I give you the author-ity...over all the power of the enemy"* (Luke 10:19). We have a right to bind his power. If a person is troubled by evil thoughts, he is safe; if he is not troubled, he is in danger.

If you are troubled by evil thoughts, test them and say, "Did Jesus come in the flesh?" That demon will go. You have a right to know these things because they will keep you in a place of real victory. If you are not troubled by evil thoughts, you need to repent and ask God to purify your hearts.

Until you voice anything, the Devil does not know it. You have desired to have converts, you have desired to have a glorious time in your meetings, and you have voiced it, and then you have had to fight as if for life and death to get it. Why? Because all the Adversary's power came. Why? Because you declared it. He would not have known if you had not declared it.

Q: Should you ask God for inspirations in secret, so that the Devil cannot know?

A: No. Always pray aloud so the Devil will clear out. When Jesus said to pray in secret (Matt. 6:6), He did not mean that you are to pray si-lently. He meant that you are to go in your prayer closet and shout aloud. If you do not, you will find that the Devil will battle you in every way; you will fall asleep, for example. Pray aloud.

Q: If a person has made the mistake of declaring his position against the Devil so that the forces of hell are arrayed against him, what will be effective in destroying Satan's power?

A: It is no mistake to declare yourself against the Devil. We are talking about two different situations here. Suppose you declare something such as this: "We are going to have the greatest time on earth. We will have a revival. We will have a time of fasting," or something similar. You have guaranteed that those will be difficult times, because Satan will assail himself against you. He cannot dethrone you, he cannot hinder you, but he will do all he can to do it. He will hinder you from having the blessing sooner. If you are fighting demon powers, there is not the same liberty as if there were no demon powers fighting you. Nevertheless, it is a good thing to have them to fight. Don't be afraid of demon powers; don't be afraid of being in temptation, because the Scriptures are clear that if you are not worthy to be tempted, you are no good. (See 2 Thessalonians 1:4–5.)

Now, suppose I came into this meeting and I said, "Jesus, in Your name I bind the powers of darkness"? It is finished. Satan won't come here. But if I declare such and such a thing without guarding myself, I will have to fight to get it.

FOURTEEN

TONGUES AND THE INTERPRETATION OF TONGUES

To another [are given] *different kinds of tongues, to another the interpretation of tongues.*
—1 Corinthians 12:10

he manifestations of tongues and the interpretation of tongues are so closely related that it would be very difficult to deal with one without the other, and I believe that it will be very profitable for you if I explain the two together.

Why tongues? Why has God brought this gift into operation? There is a reason. If there were not a reason, it would not be there.

I love the concept of "God over all, through all, in all." I love the concept that God has all power over all the powers of the Enemy—in the heavenlies, on the earth, and under the earth. Where can you go where He is not present (Ps. 139:7–12)?

Why did God design it all? You must see with me that the gift of tongues was never in evidence before the Holy Spirit came.

INTERPRETATION OF TONGUES

The Spirit leads and will direct every thought, and so bring into your hearts the fruit, until the fruit in your own life will be a manifestation that God is truly in you.

May the Lord grant that to us. That is a very important word.

The old dispensation was very wonderful in prophetic utterances. Every person, whoever he is, who receives the Holy Spirit will have prophetic utterances in the Spirit unto God or in a human language supernaturally coming forth, so that all the people will know that it is the Spirit.

This is the reason we want all the people filled with the Holy Spirit: they are to be prophetic. When a prophecy is given, it means that God has a thought, a word in season, that has never been in season before—things both new and old. The Holy Spirit brings things to pass!

So when God fulfilled the promise, when the time was appointed (and it is a wonderful appointment), the Holy Spirit came and filled the apostles. The gift that had never been in operation before came into operation that wonderful day in the Upper Room, and for the first time in all of history, men were speaking in a new order; it was not an old language, but language that was to be interpreted.

This is very profound because we recognize that God is speaking. No man understands it. The Spirit is speaking, and the Spirit opens the revelation that they will have, without adulteration; God's word flows through the whole place.

Tongues are a wonderful display of this; they are to revive the people; they are to give new depths of thought.

If you ever want to know why the Holy Spirit was greatly needed, you will find it in the third chapter of Ephesians. You will be amazed. The language is wonderful. Paul said that he was *"the least of all the saints"* (Eph. 3:8), and yet God had called him to be a *"minister"* (v. 7). His language is wonderful, and yet he felt in his heart and life that there was something greater, that the Spirit had him, and he bowed his knees unto the Father (v. 14).

You cannot find in all the Scriptures words with such profound fruit as those that ring through the verses of Paul's remarkable prayer in the Holy Spirit. He prayed *"that you may be filled with all the fullness of God"* (Eph. 3:19), and *"that you...may be able to comprehend with all the saints"* (vv. 17–18). He prayed that you may be able to ask and think, and think and ask, and that it will not only be abundantly but that it will also be *"exceeding abundantly above all that"* you can *"ask or think"* (v. 20).

There is a man closing down and the Holy Spirit praying.

INTERPRETATION OF TONGUES

To this end He brings you together that He might pour into you the hidden treasure, for it is in you. God has refined you, first cleansed you, made you just like a vessel that He might dwell in you and make all His acquaintance with you, that the Father, the Son, and the Holy Spirit should be primary over you, and you should just be exalted in Him, not in yourself, but He should have the glory.

THE REASON FOR TONGUES

You may have heard that three years ago I was in Los Angeles. God's blessing was upon those meetings. Some of you remember blessings received. But since the time I left, you have not known what I have done, because you have not been with me; you do not live with me. I might have lost anointing or favor with God. I might be like many people today who have lived holy lives and have received holy language, but now are living in a backslidden condition, a life that is not worthy of the language. There are people today who have lived holy lives, preached sanctification, and their language has been helpful, but something has come in the way. They have kept their language. They have lost their zeal and fire, but they still hold onto the language. This can take place in anyone's life. So I ask you, you who think you stand, *"take heed lest* [you] *fall"* (1 Cor. 10:12). You cannot play with this.

I would like you to know that the speaker is no good unless he judges himself every day. If I do not judge myself, I will be judged (1 Cor. 11:31). It is not sufficient for me to have your good word; I must have the Master's good word. It is no good to me if I look good to you. If there were one thing between me and God, I would not dare to come onto this platform unless I knew that God had made me holy, for they who bear the vessels of the Lord must be holy unto the Lord (Isa. 52:11). And I praise God because I know:

> His blood can make the vilest clean,
> His blood can make the vilest clean,
> His blood avails for me,
> His blood avails for me.

Holiness! Whiteness! Purity! Zeal!

INTERPRETATION OF TONGUES

"Grieve not the Holy Spirit whereby you are saved," but "let everything be done decently and in order" so that God will have preeminence in all things and Christ will reign over the house, even His house, of which He says, "Whose house you are if you hold fast the profession of your faith without doubting." So God is bringing us this morning to this holy place to bring us to see that we must only obey the Spirit.

WHEN A PROPHET IS OUT OF GOD'S WILL

As I said, you do not know what has taken place in my life since I was here. When the good people of the Angelus Temple wired to see if I could give them June or July, they did not know that I was still living in the center of God's holy will. Because I am only a man, it is possible that I may have grieved the Spirit. When I got up to speak here, what I said might have been only formal language without unction, nothing that would move the people. In this type of situation, someone in the place—and this is what tongues are for—someone in the place who is hungry for God and cannot rest because he is not getting the cream of the truth would begin travailing and groaning in the Spirit and speaking in tongues. Another person would travail in the same way, receiving the interpretation of these tongues, and would arise and give that interpretation, thus lifting the people where the prophet could not because he was out of the will of God.

TO KNOW THE MIND OF GOD

Then, you ask, what about situations in which you are preaching and prophesying and we are all getting blessed, and then we have tongues?

From time to time as I speak, I am so full of the glory and of the joy that my body is more full than my language can express. Then, instantly, the Spirit pours forth His word in tongues, and the power of God just lifts the whole place into revelation and words of life far beyond where we were.

Therefore, the church is to come together so that in the Spirit, the power of God can fall on Mary or John or William or Henry and move them, until, with the power of God moving through them, the people get the mind of God.

HOW TO USE TONGUES CORRECTLY

In the fourteenth chapter of 1 Corinthians, we have very definite instructions about tongues:

If anyone speaks in a tongue, let there be two or at the most three, each in turn, and let one

174

interpret. But if there is no interpreter, let him
keep silent in church, and let him speak to
himself and to God.   (1 Cor. 14:27–28)

There are three types of tongues, and the spiritual law concerning them is laid down in the Scriptures. But before we come to that, we must understand verse thirty-two of 1 Corinthians 14, or else there will be no success in this place: *"And the spirits of the prophets are subject to the prophets."*

YIELD TO THE HOLY SPIRIT

Unless you adhere to this word, every assembly where you are will be broken up, and you will cause trouble. Until you come to a right understanding of the Scriptures, you will never be pleasing to God. You are not to consider, under any circumstances, that, because you have a spiritual gift, it is right for you to use that gift, unless the unction of the Spirit is upon you.

You have to be very careful that you never use tongues and interpretation in confusion with prophecy. When prophecy is going forth and the truth is being heard and all the people are receiving it with joy and are being built up, then there is no room for tongues or interpretation. But just at the time when the language in my heart seems too big to express, then tongues come forth and God looses the whole thing, and we get a new purpose in that.

So you who have this wonderful gift of tongues must see to it that you never break in where the Spirit is having perfect right-of-way. But when the Spirit is working with you and you know there is a

175

line of truth that the Lord desires to express, then let the name of God be glorified.

You see, God wants everything to be in perfect order by the Spirit. That is why Paul said, *"If anyone speaks in a tongue, let there be two or at the most three"* (1 Cor. 14:27). You will never find me speaking if three have spoken before me. And you will never find me interpreting any word in tongues if three have spoken already. This is in order to keep the bonds of peace in the body so that the people will not be weary, because there are some people who have known nothing about what is right.

Unless you come to the Word of God, you will be in confusion and you will be in judgment. God does not want you to be in confusion or in judgment, but He wants you to be built up by the Scriptures, for the Scriptures are clear.

If the Lord reveals truth to me, and if I have said anything previously in relation to this that has not been absolutely scriptural, I will no longer say it. I allow God's Word to be my judge. If I find that anything I have said is not scriptural, I repent before God. As God is my Judge, I never say anything unless I believe it is the sincere truth. But if I find out later that it is not exactly in the most perfect keeping with the Word of God, I never say it again.

I believe there is a place to come to in which, after we have repented of a thing, we never have to repent of that thing anymore. I pray that God will give us that kind of superabundant revelation of common sense. It is because there is not a superabundant revelation of common sense that everybody is using nonsense. May the Lord help us to be true to God first; then, if we are true to God, we will be true to ourselves. Let God be first in the choice of our desires and our plans. Jesus must be glorified.

In 1 Corinthians 14:30 we read: *"If anything is revealed to another who sits by, let the first keep silent."* I hope that someday the church will so completely come into its beauty that if I am preaching and you have a revelation on that very thing, a deep revelation from God, and if you stand, I will stop preaching at that moment. Why? Because the Scripture says that if, when a prophet is speaking, anything is revealed to someone in the audience, let the first hold his peace and then let that other one speak.

Then the Scripture says, *"For you can all prophesy one by one, that all may learn and all may be encouraged"* (v. 31). This refers to the one who is preaching. He may be led to hold his peace while one in the midst of the congregation speaks his line of thought that is divinely appointed; then, after he finishes, another may have a prophecy, and he may get up, and so on, until you may have several who have prophesied and you have such revelations in this manner that the whole church is ablaze. I believe that God is going to help us so that we might be sound in mind, right in thought, holy in judgment, separated unto God, and one in the Spirit. Imagine all the people in this place being comforted and edified and going away from the church feeling that they have been in the presence of God, just because they have been obedient to the will of God.

Allow me to say this, and then you judge it afterward. You are not in the right place if you do not judge what I say. You are not to swallow everything I say; you are to judge everything I say by the Scriptures. But you must always use righteous judgment.

177

Righteous judgment is not judging through condemnation, but it is judging something according to the Word of God. Righteous judgment is not focused on criticism, but righteous judgment judges the truth of something. In this way, the church may receive edification so that all the people may be built up according to the Word of God. That is the right judgment.

Perhaps not everyone will affirm and believe what I have to say about this. However, I truly affirm and believe, because God has thus revealed it to me, that the words *"Let there be two or at the most three, each in turn"* (1 Cor. 14:27) mean that very often the speaker will not have finished his message after giving the first insight. So often I have seen in an assembly of believers that the first person has spoken and the Spirit of the Lord has been mightily upon him, but the anointing is such that he did not finish his message with his first insight of truth, and he realizes that he is not through with that message. He speaks in the Spirit again, and we feel that the tide is higher. Then he speaks a third time, and the tide is higher still, and then he stops.

This has led me to believe that *"each in turn"* (1 Cor. 14:27) means that one person may be permitted to speak in tongues three times in one meeting. In our conferences in England, we very often have nine utterances in tongues, but there will only be three people speaking. You can have nine, but it is not necessary unless the Lord is prompting it. Sometimes I find that the Spirit will take us through in prophecy in such a way that there will not be more than one, sometimes two people speaking. If I am correct, and I believe I am correct when I say this, when we are full of prophecy, the Spirit has taken our hearts and has moved them by His power. When this happens to me, I speak as fast as I can, but I am not expressing my own thoughts. The Holy Spirit is the thought, the language, and everything; the power of the Spirit is speaking. And when the power of the Holy Spirit is speaking like this, there is no need for tongues or interpretation because you are getting right from the throne the very language of the heart and the man. Then when the person's language gives out, the Spirit will speak and the Lord will give tongues and interpretation, and that will lift the whole place.

"At the most three." Don't say four or five, but three at the most. The Holy Spirit says it.

Now, three things are important before we go further.

THREE TYPES OF TONGUES

There are three types of tongues, and this is where the confusion comes in; this is where the people judge you, and this is where people have gone wrong.

I know, and every person who interprets tongues knows, that there is an intuition of divine appointment at this time. Every person who has been given the interpretation of tongues when they have had nothing before them except the glory of God will agree with this.

Now, the first type of tongues is when people are receiving the Holy Spirit, and they speak in tongues as an evidence of their baptism.

There is another approach to tongues when you are in a prayer meeting. You need to know exactly one thing: if you are in a prayer meeting when people are praying in the Spirit, never seek the interpretation. The Scripture declares it clearly: *"For he who speaks in a tongue does not speak to men but to God, for no one understands him; however, in the spirit he speaks mysteries"* (1 Cor. 14:2).

You will find that in a prayer meeting people will pray and speak in the Spirit, but it will be unto God and not for interpretation. Do not try to seek interpretation, for if you do you will find it is wrong. Never under any circumstances expect tongues to be interpreted where it is continually routine—the same and the same and the same. It is a spiritual language, but it is not a gift. What is it? You will find that it is adoration. It happens when the soul has been in a real definite position with God. Do not seek interpretation.

The third type of tongues is for interpretation. What type of tongues is this? *"Different kinds of tongues"* (1 Cor. 12:10). What are these *"different kinds of tongues"*? They are languages with perfect syllables. When a person gets up with a perfect language by the Spirit, you will find it is decisive, it is instructive, it is lovely to hear, it is divine in its appointment. It has to have interpretation because God is speaking to us in words that are not in our native language.

Tongues are to bring forth revelation and power in the church, to save it from lack and from being bound. Tongues and interpretation are for liberty among the people, to lift the saints and fill the place with the glory. God will open this to you; you will see what it means to have people among you full of the Spirit, and you will long to get the Spirit's mind.

THE INTERPRETATION OF TONGUES

Now, what is the interpretation of tongues? Interpretation is given by the same Spirit who moved the person with tongues. They are so moved by the power of the Spirit that they are in a place where they know that what God was burning within had to come out.

It is a common occurrence for me, after I give an interpretation, to meet people at the door as I go out who say, "Oh, that interpretation was lovely! I had it, too."

Another will come and say, "Oh, that interpretation was beautiful! I had it, you know."

I have had three in one meeting say that to me. "Oh, the interpretation was lovely! I had it."

Is it true? No. There is no truth in it at all. Why?

No interpreter has the interpretation, not one. I haven't got it myself. Then what do they have? They have the spirit of it. They knew it was the spirit of it, and they knew it was according to the mind of God. They got the sense of the knowledge that God was speaking and that it was the Spirit, and they knew it was right. The interpreter never has it. Why? Because he is in the channel where the Spirit is breathing every word. He does not get the word, the sentences and everything, ready-made. The Spirit breathes the whole thing, and the interpreter speaks as the Spirit gives utterance (Acts 2:4). So it is as divine and as original as the throne of God.

I want to show you the difference between genuine and false tongues. There are some people who get up and speak in tongues who give a little bit of tongues, and then a little more, and a little more, and they repeat themselves. Never give interpretation to such foolishness.

There are other people who get up and profess to interpret it, and they stutter and stammer, giving a word now and then. Is that interpretation? No. Do you think that the Holy Spirit is short of language? If you are stammering and stuttering and giving a word of interpretation now and then, don't believe it. It is not of God. What is it, then? People are waiting while some word in their minds comes forth, and they are giving you their minds. It is not interpretation.

I say all these things to save you from foolishness, to save you from people who want to be somebody. The Holy Spirit has shown me that all the time He is helping me, I have to be nothing. There is not a place where any man can ever be anything. It is in the death, union, and likeness of Christ that He becomes all in all. If we have not gone to death in the baptism of the Spirit, it shows me that we are altogether out of order.

The Spirit of the Lord has been speaking to you. I have felt the unction, I have realized the power, I have been speaking as fast as I could get it out, and the Spirit has given everything. For once in our lifetimes, we have been in the presence of the Holy Spirit. We have been where there has been the manifestation of the glory, where God is speaking to our hearts, where He is bringing us to a place of inhabitation in the Spirit.

We need to cherish this meeting as a holy meeting with God. See that you are built squarely on the authority of God. See that your testimony on salvation, sanctification, the gifts, the baptism, is biblical. Then you cannot be troubled by the Enemy. You will be above the Enemy; you will be able to say to the Enemy, *"Get thee behind me"* (Matt. 16:23 KJV), and he will get!

What are you ready for now? Are you ready for anything? Don't forget you have to go over the top. The top of what? The top of yourself, the top of your opinions and fancies and whims and foolish acts. You have to dethrone them; you have to have a biblical building; you have to be in the Scriptures. *"For God has not given us a spirit of fear, but of power and of love and of a sound mind"* (2 Tim. 1:7).

When people say to me, "Oh, I have nervous symptoms; I have a nervous weakness," I know immediately that only one thing is wrong. What is it? It is a lack of knowing the Word. *"Perfect love casts out fear."* And there is no torment, no fear, in love (1 John 4:18).

I want you to get the Word of God into your heart until the demon power has no power over you. You are over the powers of fear. Then I want you to understand that the baptism of the Holy Spirit is a love beyond any you have ever had; you are to have power after the Holy Spirit comes, and it is power over the Enemy, over yourself, and over your human mind. Self has to be dethroned, Christ has to be enthroned, and the Holy Spirit has to enlarge His position.

Go over the top and never slide down again the back way. If you go, you go forward, and you go into victory from victory, triumphing over the Enemy, having liberty in your captivity (see Ephesians 4:8), rightly rejoicing in the triumph of God.

Faith is the victory (1 John 5:4). Faith is the operation in your heart. Faith is the stimulation of the life of the Master. When you stand in faith, you are in a position in which God can take you to the place where you are *"over all"* (Luke 10:19) by the power of God.

Believe that no power of the Enemy will have power over you. Rebuke him. Stand on the authority of the Word and go forth into victory. I want you to be saved, healed, and blessed through what God's Word says.

FIFTEEN

THE PURPOSE OF TONGUES

*I thank my God I speak with tongues more than you
all; yet in the church I would rather speak five words
with my understanding, that I may teach others also,
than ten thousand words in a tongue.*
—1 Corinthians 14:18–19

his Scripture has been greatly misunder-
stood. Here the apostle Paul was saying
that he spoke in tongues more than any
others. Now, you can understand that he
felt he spoke in tongues more than all of them,
meaning that he lived in the utterances of the Spirit.
Very likely, this would be lovely!

I remember one time in London when I asked
for a meeting to commence at 7:30 P.M. I was not
well acquainted with London, and I knew I had two
hours to spare before the meeting. I was walking in
one of the busiest places in London; all the theaters
were just getting ready for their big Saturday night.

"Now, Lord," I said, "let me just be enveloped in
Your glory for these two hours in the midst of the
world."

And I went up and down Fleet Street and the Strand, lost in the Spirit, in tongues the whole time. It was lovely. Yes, the world was filled with *"the lust of the flesh, the lust of the eyes, and the pride of life"* (1 John 2:16), but God had His child in the midst of these blazing worldly affairs, lost in the Spirit.

I want you, I implore you, beloved, to desire earnestly to be in God's will so that at any time, wherever you are, you may pray in the Spirit, you may sing in the Spirit, you may have a good time thinking about the Lord. Remember that it is at these places and times and seasons when the Father and the Son come and make themselves known to you.

Now, a word in season regarding the next point. Paul knew that if the whole church turned to tongues, and tongues only—tongues! tongues! tongues!—there would be confusion and much distress, and there would not be that lift of divine power and fellowship that Paul knew was needed.

So Paul's great heart as a builder of churches was moved; he saw that the Lord was breathing through him this glorious desire to form these churches, and he said to the Corinthians, in effect, "Think seriously, and let your speaking be with carefulness. The people who have been filled with the Spirit and speak in tongues should not go on constantly with that; they should not come to the meeting and continually have it taken up with speaking in tongues."

You know, the flow of the Spirit through you is very lovely; yes, it is very lovely, but we must always be mindful that our brother and sister sitting next to us have to be helped. There are weak people in the church who need your careful attention. Then there are people of different kinds of temperament and makeup. We must always remember that we have to guard the church, look after it, keep it with sober mind, until no person coming in may be taken up with the thought, "Why, these people are mad! There they are, all speaking in tongues." (See 1 Corinthians 14:23.)

Paul said, "I would rather speak five words with my understanding than ten thousand words that they couldn't understand." (See verse 19.)

Wasn't he right? Wouldn't I prefer the same thing? Is there anybody who is really in wisdom who would dare to continue speaking in tongues without interpretation and without opening the knowledge of God to the people? Who would dare to do that? It would be foolishness, it would be madness, and you would lose the opinion of the people.

You need to remember that whatever you do when you are in the church of God, you must seek to excel to the edifying of the body of Christ.

TONGUES, A SIGN TO THE UNBELIEVER

There is a word here that says that tongues are *"a sign"* for the unbeliever: *"Therefore tongues are for a sign, not to those who believe but to unbelievers"* (1 Cor. 14:22). We have a wonderful word there, and I know it will require some explanation. It is important, and I want to explain it so that it edifies you.

A friend of mine was attending a Wesleyan brotherhood meeting in England, a large, packed meeting. He saw a young man there who was full of desire for the salvation of his people. He looked it, and his body posture and his face looked it. My friend knew he was laboring there under great difficulty.

At the close of the service, he wrote him a check. He said, "Take this check and go to Bradford to Brother Wigglesworth, a friend of mine, and have a rest in his home. All you have to do is to say that I have sent you. They will take you in and make you comfortable."

When this young man got the check, he was in need of a rest, and he said to my friend, "Yes, I will go, and I thank you."

He arranged to go the next Friday. The first thing he did when he got to Bradford was to go to the Young Men's Christian Association to inquire if they knew anything about Wigglesworth.

"Oh, yes, we know everything about him. Why?"

"I have brought a letter of introduction to him and have been advised to go to his home for a rest."

"Now, you be very careful," they said. "This man is among those people who believe in tongues, and we believe it is of the Devil. So you be careful lest you be taken in."

"Oh!" he said. "Don't be afraid; they will not take me in. I am too wise for that."

So he came.

I want you to notice that the Scripture passage we are dealing with now is about tongues as an evidence to the unbeliever—not to the believer but to the unbeliever.

This man came to my house full of unbelief. He is a great preacher and a wonderful man with great abilities, and I tell you—I know him well—that he is a godly man. But he was full of unbelief.

There are any number of people who are believers filled with unbelief. I have very little difficulty when I am dealing with a sinner about being healed. I scarcely ever see a sinner who knows nothing about Jesus fail to be healed when I pray for him. But if I pray for a believer, I very often find that he is not healed. Why? There is unbelief in the believer. It is a very astounding thing.

God speaks in the old prophetic language nine times as much to the backslider as He does to the sinner. So I want you to know there is no place for you except to only believe what God says. When you come to that place, God will bless you; you will be amazed at how much He will bless you.

INTERPRETATION OF TONGUES

For God has not chosen you that He might make you as a waster, but He has chosen you to bring you on the hill of perfection, that you might know that there will not be weakness in you but strength and character, for God has chosen you.

This message is for someone in the meeting: "God has chosen you." Do not be afraid. God has chosen you.

To resume my story, when the young man got to my house, my wife was in the house alone. He went in and he talked, and talked, and talked, and talked. When I got home, my wife came out and said to me, "We have the strangest man we ever had in our house. He has been in there for half an hour, and he has never stopped talking. You never heard such a talker."

"Let him alone," I said. "He will come to an end."

I was introduced to him, and he went on talking. He talked through the dinner hour and right through to nighttime.

That night we were having a meeting at our house. He didn't stop talking. He knew that if he stopped, he would allow something else into his mind, so he was going to talk and block everyone else who talked. He wasn't willing to be taken in with this.

The meeting began to fill up; the room was packed.

"Brother," I said, "you have talked ever since you came. We are now going to pray. It is our meeting night; you must cease to speak."

He got down before God. My, it was wonderful! The power of God fell upon us, and something happened that never happened before, as far as I can remember. We always began our meeting with a song—always—but this time we began it in an attitude of prayer.

At one side of the fireplace knelt one young woman and at the other side of the fireplace knelt another. I have never known it to happen before or since, but, deliberately, instead of praying, those two began speaking in tongues.

As soon as they began speaking in tongues, this man jumped up, startled. He ran to the one nearest him, his hands on his ears, and bent down over the girl; then frantically he ran to the other, then back to the first, then to the other one.

Finally he came and said to me, "Can I go to my room?"

"Yes, Brother."

He was shown to his room.

We had a wonderful meeting. At about 3:30 the next morning, he came to my door and knocked.

"May I come in?" he called.

"Yes," I said. "Come in."

As soon as he got in, he stammered, "Bl—bl—bl—" with his hand to his mouth. "It's come! It's come!"

"Go back to bed, Brother," I said.

The next morning he came down to breakfast.

"Oh, wasn't that a wonderful night!" he exclaimed.

"Which do you mean?" I asked.

We had had a wonderful time. I wanted to know what he had done.

"Oh!" he said. "When I came here, I heard in Bradford that you had received the power of the working of evils; I was warned to keep away, and I was filled with unbelief. I was determined that nothing of that would affect me. I made up my mind that I would talk every moment. But when you told the people to go to prayer, the moment those people began speaking in tongues, I went to them. I know Greek and I know Hebrew, and one was saying to me in Greek, 'Get right with God,' and the other was saying in Hebrew, 'Get right with God.'"

Oh, yes, God has a way to do it, and God can do it. When we get unbelief out of the way, the baptism of fire, revelation, the gifts of the Spirit, the harmony, the comfort, the blessed unction will abound until there will never be a dry meeting; every meeting will be filled with life and power and joy in the Holy Spirit.

Continuing his story, this man said, "When I heard that, I knew it was for me. I went upstairs and I repented. I knew I had been wrongly interpreting what God meant, and I repented. As I repented, I found myself overcome by the power of the Spirit. I tried to resist, but God was dealing with me in such a way that I fell down under the power of the Spirit over and over, until God sanctified me. At 3:30 the power of God fell upon me. I found myself speaking as the Spirit gave utterance, and I came to your door."

That man is a wonderful man today. God has blessed him everywhere.

SIXTEEN

A More Excellent Way

raise the Lord! The Word of God is very clear regarding this: *"Let everything that has breath praise the LORD. Praise the LORD!"* (Ps. 150:6). If you ever get to the place where you cannot praise the Lord, it is a calamity in your life and it is a calamity to the people who are around you. If you want to take blessing into homes and make all the people around you know that you have something more than an ordinary life, you must know that God has come to supplant you and put within you a perfect praise.

God has a great place for us, so that His will may be done and we may be subject to His perfect will. When that comes to pass, no one can tell what may happen, for Jesus reached the highest place when He said, *"For I have come down from heaven, not to do My own will, but the will of Him who sent Me"* (John 6:38). So there is something in a place of yielding where God can have us for His own.

God has a choice for us all so that we might lose ourselves in God in a way we have never done before. I want to provoke you to love so that you will come into a place of blessing, for God wants you to be blessed so that you will be a blessing.

Beloved, believe today that God has a way for you. Perhaps you have never come that way before. God has a way beyond all your ways of thought. He has a choice and a plan for you.

There is a great need today. People are hungry for truth. People are thirsting, wanting to know God better. There are thousands *"in the valley of decision"* (Joel 3:14), wanting someone to take them right into the depths of God.

Are you ready to pray? You say, "What should I ask for?"

You may not know what to ask for, but if you begin, the Spirit knows the desire of your heart, and He will pray according to the mind of God. You do not know, but God knows everything, and He is acquainted with you altogether and desires to promote you.

So I say, "Are you ready?" You say, "What for?" Are you ready to come promptly into the presence of God so that you may ask this day as you have never asked before? Ask in faith, nothing doubting, believing that God is on the throne waiting to anoint you afresh today.

Are you ready? What for? Are you ready to be brought into the banquet house of God, even as Esther came in before King Ahasuerus? God will put out the scepter, and all that your heart desires He will give to you. (See Esther 5–7.)

Father, in Jesus' name we come before You believing in Your almightiness, that the power of Your hand does move us, chasten us. Build us. Let the Word of God sink into our hearts this day. Make us,

O God, worthy of the name we bear, that we may go about as real, holy saints of God. Just as if You were on the earth, fill us with Your anointing, Your power, and Your grace. Amen.

HUMILITY AND COMPASSION

It is very important to minister in the gifts of the Spirit in the proper way. What a serious thing it would be, after waiting for the enduement of power for months and months and months, to fail God because we turned to some human desire just because we liked it.

I want to say at the beginning that there is no anointing like the unction that comes out of death, when we are dead with Christ. It is that position that makes us live with Him. If we have been conformed to His death, then, in that same death, like Paul, we will be made like Him in His resurrection power (Phil. 3:10–11).

But do not forget that Jesus was coequal with the Father and that He made Himself of no reputation when he became man and came to earth (Phil. 2:6–7). He did not come out and say that He was this, that, or the other. No, that was not His position. Jesus had all the gifts. He could have stood up and said to Peter and John and James and the rest of them, when the dead son was being carried through the gate of the city of Nain (see Luke 7:11–15), "Stand to one side, Peter. Clear out of the way, John. Make room for Me, Thomas. Don't you know who I am? I am coequal with the Father. I have all power, I have all gifts, I have all graces. Stand to one side; I will show you how to raise the dead!"

Is that how He did it? No! Never. Then what made it come to pass?

He was observant. The disciples were there, but they did not have the same observance. Observance comes from an inward holy flame kindled by God.

What did He see? He saw the widow and knew that she was carrying to burial that day all her help, all her life. Her love was bound up in that son. There she was, broken and bent over with sorrow, all her hopes blighted.

Jesus had compassion upon her, and the compassion of Jesus was greater than death. His compassion was so marvelous that it went beyond the powers of death and all the powers of demons.

"Bless the LORD, O my soul, and forget not all His benefits" (Ps. 103:2). Isn't He a lovely Jesus! Isn't He a precious Savior! Don't you see that if we bear in our body the marks of Jesus (Gal. 6:17) or the life of the manifestation of Jesus, if we live only as Jesus is manifested, if people realize that we have *"been with Jesus"* (Acts 4:13), as they realized it of Peter and John, then that would pay for everything? Oh, it would surely be beautiful!

PRESUMPTION

These meetings are not ordinary meetings. The Holy Spirit is among us; Jesus is being glorified. We are not seeking our own in these meetings, but we are seeking to provoke one another to holiness and character (Heb. 10:24) so that we may be of the same mind as Jesus. The same manifestation that was in Him has to be in us.

196

I must never, under any circumstances, as long as I live, take advantage of God or Jesus or the Holy Spirit. I have to be subservient to the power of God.

Let me give you a little illustration that will help you in thinking about this.

One day a young man got very elated because he had received the baptism in the Holy Spirit, and he got into a place that most people seemed to fail to see was the wrong place. This young man was on the platform during a meeting, and he said, "I am baptized with the Holy Spirit. I can cast out devils. Come, I can cast them out!"

There was a poor man there who had been bound by the Devil for many, many years, so bound that he was helpless. He could not help himself; he was bound in every way. He had never heard such words before, and when he heard them he was so moved that he struggled out of his seat, took hold of the chairs, and went down among the people in the aisle. He was a poor helpless man who was seeking relief the first time he heard that he could be delivered.

He went up and stood before the preacher and cried out, "Cast them out! Please cast them out! Help me; please cast them out!"

The young man did all he could, but he could not do it. The church was broken, the whole place was brought into travail. Oh, they wept and they cried because it was not done.

A PERFECT WAY

It never will be done that way. That isn't the way to do it. But there is a way to minister in all the gifts of the Spirit, and it is the way that is in the Scriptures. Let us look into this perfect way that is found in 1 Corinthians 13, starting with the first verse:

Though I speak with the tongues of men and of angels, but have not love, I have become sounding brass or a clanging cymbal.

Did you ever read a verse like this? It is the state of being brought into a treasury. Do you know what a treasury is? A treasury holds or handles priceless things.

God puts you into the treasury to hold or handle the precious gifts of the Spirit. Therefore, so that you may not fail to handle them correctly, He gives you a picture of how you may handle them.

What a high position of authority, of grace, the Lord speaks about in this verse! *"Speak with the tongues of men and of angels."* Oh, isn't that wonderful!

There are men who have such wonderful qualifications for speaking. Their knowledge in the natural realm is so surpassing that many people go to hear their eloquent addresses because the language in them is so beautiful. Yet, through the baptism in the Holy Spirit, God puts you right in the midst of them and says that He has given you the capability to speak like men, with power of thought and language at your disposal, so that you can say anything.

People are failing God all the time all over the world because they are taken up with their own eloquence, and God is not in it. They are lost with the pretentiousness of their great authority over language, and they use it on purpose to tickle the ears and the sensations of the people, and it profits nothing. It is nothing. It will wither up, and the people who use it will wither up.

Yet God has said there is a way. Now, how would language *of men and of angels* (1 Cor. 13:1) come to prosper?

When you wept through to victory before, you were able to do anything. You were so undone that unless God helped you to do it, you couldn't do it. You were so broken in spirit that your whole body seemed to be at an end unless God reinstated you. Then the unction came, and every word was glorifying Jesus. Every sentence lifted the people, and they felt as they listened, "Surely God is in this place! He has sent His Word and healed us" (see Psalm 107:20). They saw no man there except Jesus. Jesus was so manifested that they all said, "Oh, wasn't Jesus speaking to our hearts this morning!"

If you minister in this way, you will never become nothing. Tongues of men and angels alone will come to nothing. Yet if you speak with tongues of men and angels that are bathed in the love of God until it is to Him alone that you speak, then it will be written down forever in the history of the glory.

Never think for a moment that the Acts of the Apostles has been completed. It is an incomplete book. When you read Revelation, it is complete. You cannot add to nor take from this wonderful truth of prophecy. It is complete. And so, when you are used only for and desire only the glory of God, your acts and life, ministry, and power will be an endless recording in the glory of heaven—for the Acts of the Apostles are being recorded in the glory.

So let the Lord help us to know how to act in the Holy Spirit.

INTERPRETATION OF TONGUES

Set your house in order, for unless you die, you cannot live. For God is coming today and taking us—others may be left, but we are taken—taken on with God, taken into God, moved by the power of God, until we live and move in God and God has us as His channel, breathing through, divinely fixing, bringing forth words new and old. And God is moving in the midst, and His people are being fed with the finest of the wheat.

We have a great salvation, but some people limit it. I believe in eternal salvation. The question has been asked me, "Do you believe that after you are saved, you are forever saved?" The Scriptures are very clear on this, and they are the words of Jesus. What does He say? *"My sheep hear My voice, and I know them, and they follow Me"* (John 10:27).

I do not believe that you are a sheep if you do not follow. But if you follow, you are all right; if you do not follow, it shows you were never right. So if you are all right, you will remain right and you will end up right.

Do not forget that it is only those who hear His voice who belong to the fold. And so, if you are acting indiscreetly, carelessly, frivolously, and sinfully, you have never been in it; you are a stranger to it. *"My sheep hear My voice...and they follow Me."* They will not listen to the voice of a stranger, and they have not turned aside to everything else. They live—and, oh, it is a lovely life—they live in the will of God.

PROPHECY AND GOODNESS

Let us look at the second verse from 1 Corinthians 13:

And though I have the gift of prophecy, and understand all mysteries and all knowledge, and though I have all faith, so that I could remove mountains, but have not love, I am nothing.

This second verse is like the first, only the Word of God is very remarkable. It starts like this, brings you to a place where there is no condemnation, and then fills you up where there is no separation. That is God's plan.

Lots of people desire to have faith; lots of people desire to have prophecy; lots of people long to know mysteries. Who knows mysteries? *"The secret of the LORD is with those who fear Him"* (Ps. 25:14). Don't change the Scriptures. *"The just shall live by faith"* (Rom. 1:17). Do not alter the Scriptures. It takes a just man to live by faith.

Do not forget that prophecy is beautiful when you understand the principle of it. Prophecy is the sixth gift mentioned in 1 Corinthians 12. What fruit or grace do you think would coincide with prophecy? Why, goodness, of course.

Why goodness? Because if you are living in holiness, entire sanctification, perfection, you would never take advantage of the Holy Spirit and would speak only as the Spirit gave prophecy. You would never say human things just because you had the gift of prophecy. You would speak according to the Spirit, giving prophecy because you had been holy.

When you speak in the natural after you have received the gift of prophecy, it is because you have come to be nothing; you are nothing; you are not counted in the great plan of the great purpose of God. But if you are hidden in Christ and your whole heart is perfected in God, and you will prophesy only when the Spirit of the Lord is upon you, then it will be something that lasts forever. People will be blessed forever and God will be glorified forever.

FAITH WITHOUT LOVE

Suppose that I have all faith so that I could move mountains. Now, suppose that I also have a big farm, but that some of my farmland is not very profitable. It is stony; it has many rocks on it as well as some little mountains that are absolutely untillable and do no good. But because I have faith without love, I say, "I will use my faith and I will move this land. I do not care where it goes as long as my land is clean."

So I use my faith to clear my land. The next day, my poor next-door neighbor comes and says, "I am in great trouble. All your wasteland and stony, rocky land has been tipped onto mine, and my good land is ruined."

And I, who have faith without love, say to him, "You get faith and move it back!"

That profits nothing. If God brings you into a place of faith, let it be for the glory of God. Then, when you pray, God will wonderfully answer you; nothing will hinder your being used for God, for God delights to use us.

Gifts are not only given; they are also increased to those who can be used, who can keep in a place of useableness. God keeps these yielded ones in a place of being continually supplanted—a new place that is deeper, higher, holier, richer, more heavenly.

In addition, gifts are not only useable, but God is also glorified in Jesus when you pray the prayer of faith. Jesus Himself said, "When you pray believing, the Father will be glorified in the Son." (See John 14:12–13.)

SACRIFICE NOTHING WITHOUT LOVE

We will move on now to the third verse:

And though I bestow all my goods to feed the poor, and though I give my body to be burned, but have not love, it profits me nothing.
(1 Cor. 13:3)

Though I have such means that I can lay my hands on millions of dollars, though I can do all kinds of things with the money, and though, after I have given it all, I show the people more by giving my body to be burned, saying, "I will show the people what kind of material I am made of!" this is nothing, nothing! Your gifts will perish unless the gifts are used for the glory of Jesus. Five dollars given in the name of the Lord is of more value than thousands without acknowledging Him.

A man came to me, and we had long talks about the workings of the Lord. He told me, "I was in a very difficult place. I had been working very hard in the church and had given all my strength...."

Oh, I see such godly, holy people doing more than they ought to, thereby giving themselves away. Don't you know that your body belongs to God (1 Cor. 6:19–20), and that, if you overtax your body, God says He will judge you for it? We have to be careful because the body that is given to us is to exhibit His power and His glory, and we cannot do this if we give ourselves all the time to work, work, work, work, work and think that that is the only way. It is not the way.

The Scriptures teach us that Jesus had to go and renew His spiritual vision and power in solitude with His Father (Mark 1:35), and it was also necessary for the disciples to draw aside and rest awhile (6:30–31). Couldn't Jesus give them all they needed? My dear brother, whatever God gives you, He will never take away your common sense.

Suppose I unwisely overextended my body and knew that I had done so? How could I ask anyone to pray for me unless I repented? We must be careful. Our bodies are the temples of the Holy Spirit, and He has to dwell in them, and they have to be for His purpose in the world. We are not working for ourselves; God is to be glorified in our bodies. Lots of people today are absolutely withered up, years before their time, because they went beyond their knowledge. But dare to believe.

Let me tell you a personal story to illustrate this. In 1914 the Lord moved upon me in England to tell the people that I was going to America, coming in through Canada.

"Well, Lord," I said, "You know You will have to do a miracle, and You must do it sharp if You mean business, because I want to be in haste about this if it is Your plan. The first thing is that, as you know, I have a bad memory. You will have to work a miracle there. The next thing is that You will have to find me all the money because I cannot leave my children without money, and I have no money to go, so You will have to find a lot."

It was amazing how the Lord began to provide it. It was coming so fast that I said to the people, "Oh, the Lord has sent so much money that I am sure I am going!"

Then He stopped. There was no more money.

"Lord! Lord!" I said, "I know I have grieved You, and I repent. If You begin again to show me it is Your will, I won't tell anybody."

And it commenced again, falling as gently as rain.

My boy said to me, "Father, Mother has gone to heaven. If you go on this trip, it will be very lonely for me without you."

The front doorbell rang. I said to him, "George, go answer the front door, and let the Lord speak to you through this ring at the door whether I have to go or not."

There was a letter.

"Now, George," I said, "open that letter, and whatever is in the letter, read it, and let that suffice you whether I have to go or not."

George opened the letter. That letter had been traveling for six weeks; it began coming just about the time I repented. In it was a check for twenty-five pounds.

"What about it, George?" I asked.

"Oh!" he said. "Father, I won't say anything else."

I was rushing onto the ship one day not long afterward, when a poor woman who was dressed very shabbily, and whom I didn't know, came and gave me a big red sugar bag. I was packed with things, and I couldn't say a word to her because there were so many people to see me off and everything, so I just put the bag on one side. When the ship began moving, I thought, "Well, I will look in the sugar bag."

And there were twenty-five gold coins! Can't He provide it!

Beloved, let the Lord do things. He knows how to do them.

Because I felt that my coming to America and Canada was all the Lord's doing, I said, "Lord, I will never let an opportunity slip." I traveled at night to preach at day, took advantage of every opportunity, went so far that I got to the point that I could not eat.

After one meeting, the people said, "You have lifted the meeting, lifted the meeting."

"Yes," I said, "God is with us."

They went to eat, but I could not. Then they said to me, "Wigglesworth, you do not understand your body. You are helping everybody in the Spirit, but your body has gotten so run down that if you do not go home, you may never be able to come back."

Ah! I had zeal without knowledge (Rom. 10:2); I had a love for God, but there was no wisdom in it. God showed me that if I would take care of my body, He could use me for years and years to come, and I find today that I am stronger and better and more ready for action than I was thirty years ago.

INTERPRETATION OF TONGUES
For it is the Lord your God "who opens and no man shuts." When He blesses, it will surely

tend to blessing. And remember this, God has not called you in to keep your face down; He has called you in to laden you with the treasures and then pass you out to scatter the good things. God is at the right hand of those people who are seeking diligently only to follow Him, for God has set His heart upon you. David says, "When I was poor and needy, then the Lord thought about me." It is in the poverty of our weaknesses that God becomes the refreshing and strength of our human nature and spiritual quality and keeps us in the earth, fresh and ready.

Oh, Father, we do thank you for this!

Beloved, make sure that you see to these things. God will give you faith. God will give you prophecies. God will give gifts. And remember this, God will enrich you.

Did you ever know a time in your life when you were poorer after you began to serve the Lord? No. God blesses in basket and store, and He blesses in the body. It pays to serve the Lord in holiness, for God has a purpose in it. It is when you get out of the will of God that you have a hard time. Let God's will be done. There is money that *"leads to poverty"* (Prov. 11:24), and there are gifts of God that bring you into riches. So I implore you to serve God with all your heart.

I had hoped to go deeper into this thirteenth chapter of 1 Corinthians, but if we had gone deeper, we would not have come out again. There are many things to say about this chapter. For instance, how beautiful it would be to know what this really means: *"Love suffers long and is kind"* (1 Cor. 13:4).

I do not have time for any more, except this: the time is not past for much more. It is past for any more from me, but you are on the threshold of much more from God. May the Lord bless you in such a way that you will be in a place where God will be at your right hand (Ps. 16:8).

Faith is an act; faith is a leap; faith jumps in; faith claims. Faith has an author, and faith's author is Jesus. He is the Author and the Finisher of faith (Heb. 12:2).

Now, how much do you dare to ask for? How much do you dare to imagine? How much do you dare to expect will come? How much? May I move you to this banquet, this place of treasure, this "much more," this "abundant," this "abounding," this "exceeding"? (See Ephesians 3:20.) Jump up into God. Dare to believe. Faith is enough; ask and believe.

Give me grace, Lord—anyhow, any way—only have Your way.

SEVENTEEN

LOVE AND THE GIFTS

hank God for the Word that comes to us afresh! Early this morning I was thinking and wondering if the Lord would speak through me, and I was strongly impressed that I should read to you 1 Corinthians 13.

I am so thankful to God that He has dovetailed this thirteenth chapter of 1 Corinthians between the twelfth and the fourteenth. The twelfth chapter deals expressly with the gifts of the Spirit, and the fourteenth chapter is on the lines of the manifestations and the gifts of the Spirit; the thirteenth chapter functions similarly to the governor balls that control a steam engine. If you ever see this type of engine working, you will find that right over the main valve that lets in the steam, there are two little balls that go around. Often they go as fast as they can, though sometimes they go slowly. They open and shut the valve that sends the steam to the pistons. These are constructed so that the engine does not get out of control.

I find that God, the Holy Spirit, in His remarkable wisdom, has placed the thirteenth chapter right between these wonderful chapters on the gifts that we love to dwell upon so much. How wonderful, how magnificent they are! God has given them to us so that we may be useful, not ornamental, and prove in every case and under every circumstance that we might be available at the right time with these gifts. They are enduement for power; they are expressive of His love; they are for the edification and comfort of so many weary souls.

We find that God brings these gifts in perfect order so that the church may receive blessings. Yet how many people, how many of us, have failed to come to the summit of perfection because the governor balls were not working well, because we were more taken up with the gift than the power that moved the gift, because we were more frequently delighted in the gift than the Giver of the gift! Then the gift became fruitless and helpless, and we were sorry. Sometimes it brought on rebuke, and sometimes we suffered, suffered more or suffered less.

INTERPRETATION OF TONGUES

The love that constrains, the grace that adorns, the power that sustains, the gift that remains may be in excellence, when He is the Governor, the Controller, the Worker.

I do thank God for tongues and interpretation, because they introduce new vision; they open the larger avenue. Let it please You today, Lord, to show us how to work and how to walk and not stumble.

THE GIFTS

Now, beloved, the topic of love and the gifts is a very large one. However, I will do all I can, by the grace of God, so that I may say things that will live after I have gone away. For it is very necessary that we receive the Holy Spirit in the first place; after receiving the Holy Spirit, we must earnestly desire the gifts. Then, after receiving the gifts, we must never forget that the gift is entrusted to us for bringing the blessings of God to the people.

For instance, divine healing is a gift for ministering to the needs of the people. The gift of wisdom is a word in season at the moment of need, to show you just what to do. The gift of knowledge, or the word of knowledge, is to inspire you because of the consecutiveness of the Word of God, to bring you life and joy. This is what God intends.

Then there is the gift of discernment. We are not to discern one another, but to discern evil powers and deal with them and command them back to the pit from which they came. Regarding the gift of miracles, God intends for us to come to the place where we will see miracles worked. God also wants us to understand that tongues are profitable only when they exalt and glorify the Lord. And oh, that we might really know what it means when interpretation is given! It is not merely to have beautiful sensations and think that is interpretation, but it is such that the man who has it does not know what is coming, for if he did, it would not be interpretation. Interpretation is not knowing what you are going to say, but it is being in the place where you say exactly what God says. So when I have to interpret a message, I purposely keep my mind from anything that would hinder, and I sometimes say "Praise the Lord" and "Hallelujah" so that everything will be a word through the Spirit, and not my word, but the word of the Lord!

Now I understand that we can have these divine gifts so perfectly balanced by divine love that they will be a blessing all the time. However, there is sometimes such a desire in the flesh to do something attention-getting. How the people listen and long for divine prophecy, just as interpretation comes forth. How it thrills! There is nothing wrong with it; it is beautiful. We thank God for the office and the purpose that has caused it to come, but let us be careful to finish when we are through and not continue on our own. That is how prophecy is spoiled. If you continue on your own, at the end of the anointing, you are using false fire; at the end of the message, you will try to continue. Don't fail, beloved, because the people know the difference. They know what is full of life, what is the real thing.

Then again, it is the same with a person praying. We love people to pray in the Holy Spirit; how we love to hear them pray even the first sentences because the fire is there. However, what spoils the most holy person in prayer is when, after the spirit of prayer has gone forth, he continues on and people say, "I wish he would stop," and the church becomes silent. They say, "I wish that brother would stop. How beautifully he began; now he is dry!" But he doesn't stop.

A preacher was once having a wonderful time, and the people enjoyed it, but when he was through, he continued. A man came and said to someone at the door, "Has he finished?" "Yes," said the man, "long since, but he won't stop!" May God save us from that. People know when you are praying in the Spirit. Why should you take time and spoil everything because the natural side has come into it? God never intended that. God has a supernatural side; that is the true side, and how beautiful it is! People sometimes know better than we do, and we would also know if we were more careful.

May the Lord grant us revelation; we need discernment; we need intuition. It is the life inside. It is salvation inside, cleansing, filling; it is all inside. Revelation is inside. It is for exhibition outside, but always remember that it is inside. God's Son said as much when He said, "The pure in heart will see God." (See Matthew 5:8.) There is an inward sight of God, and it is the pure in heart who see God.

Lord, keep us pure so that we will never block the way.

LOVE

Love is always in the place of revelation.

Though I speak with the tongues of men and of angels, but have not love, I have become sounding brass or a clanging cymbal. And though I have the gift of prophecy, and understand all mysteries and all knowledge, and though I have all faith, so that I could remove mountains, but have not love, I am nothing.

(1 Cor. 13:1–2)

Now, it is a remarkable fact that God intends us to be examples of the truth. These are divine truths, and God intends us to be examples of these truths. Beloved, it is lovely to be in the will of God. Now then, how may we be something? By just being nothing, by receiving the Holy Spirit, by being in the

213

place where you can be operated by God and filled with the power to operate.

What it must be to have speaking ability, to have a beautiful language, as so many men have! There are men who are wonderful in language. I used to like to read Talmadge when he was alive; how his messages used to inspire me. But, oh, this divine power! It is wonderful to have the tongue of an angel so that all the people who hear you are moved by your use of language. Yet how I would weep, how my heart would be broken, if I came to speak before you in beautiful language without the power!

If I had an angel's language and the people were all taken with what I said, but Jesus was not glorified at all, it would all be hopeless, barren, and unfruitful. I myself should be nothing. But if I speak and say, "Lord, let them hear Your voice. Lord, let them be compelled to hear Your truth. Lord, anyhow, any way, hide me today," then He becomes glorious, and all the people say, "We have seen Jesus!"

When I was in California, I spent many days with our dear Brother Montgomery when I had a chance. During this time, a man wrote to Brother Montgomery. This man had been saved but had lost his joy; he had lost all he had. He wrote, "I am through with everything. I am not going to touch this thing again; I am through." Brother Montgomery wrote back to him and said, "I will never try to persuade you again if you will hear once. There is a man from England, and if you will only hear him once, I will pay all your expenses." So he came. He listened, and at the end of the time he said to me, "This is the truth I am telling you. I have seen the

Lord standing beside you, and I heard His voice. I never even saw you.

"I have a lot of money," he continued, "and I have a valley five hundred miles long. If you speak the word to me, I will go on your word, and I will open that valley for the Lord."

I have preached in several of his places, and God has used him wonderfully to speak throughout that valley. What I would have missed when he came the first day, if I had been trying to say something of my own instead of the Lord being there and speaking His words through me! Never let us do anything to lose this divine love, this close affection in our hearts that says, "Not I, but Christ; not I, but Christ!"

I want to say, "Forget yourself and get lost in Him." Lose all your identity in the Son of God. Let Him become all in all. Seek only the Lord, and let Him be glorified. You will have gifts; you will have grace and wisdom. God is waiting for the person who will lay all on the altar, fifty-two weeks in the year, three hundred and sixty-five days in the year, and then continue perpetually in the Holy Spirit.

I would have liked to have gone on with this topic. I have such joy in this. Beloved, go on for every blessing from the Lord, so that the Lord will be large in you, so that the wood and the hay and the stubble will be burned up (1 Cor. 3:12–13 KJV), and the Lord will bring you to a great harvesttime. Now, beloved, shall we not present ourselves to the Lord so that He may put His hand upon us and say, "My child, my child, be obedient to the message; hear what the Spirit says to you so that you may go on and possess the land"? The Lord will give you a great inheritance.

EIGHTEEN

A Final Word About the Gifts

Even so you, since you are zealous for spiritual gifts,
let it be for the edification of the church
that you seek to excel.
—1 Corinthians 14:12

his Scripture is the Word of God, and it is most important that when we read the Word, we do so with hearts that have purposed to obey its every precept. We have no right to open the Word of God carelessly or indifferently. I have no right to come to you with any message unless it is absolutely in the perfect order of God. I believe we are in order to consider further the subject that we greatly need to be informed about in these days. So many people are receiving the baptism of the Holy Spirit, but then they do not know which way to go.

We have a great need today. It is that we may be supplied with revelation according to the mind of the Lord, that we may be instructed by the mind of the

217

Spirit, that we may be able to rightly divide the Word of Truth (2 Tim. 2:15), and that we may not be novices, considering the fact that the Spirit of the Lord has come to us in revelation. We ought to be alert to every touch of divine, spiritual illumination.

We should carefully consider what the apostle Paul said to us: *"Do not grieve the Holy Spirit of God, by whom you were sealed for the day of redemption"* (Eph. 4:30). The sealing of the Spirit is very remarkable, and I pray to God that not one of you may lose the divine inheritance that God has chosen for you, which is greater than you could choose if your mind had ten times its normal faculties. God's mind is greater than yours. His thoughts are higher than the heavens over you (Isa. 55:9), so that you do not need to be afraid.

I have great love for my sons in England, great love for my daughter here; but it is nothing in comparison to God's love toward us. God's love wants us to walk up and down the earth as His Son did: clothed, filled, radiant, with fire beaming forth from our countenances, setting forth the power of the Spirit so that the people jump into liberty.

But there is deplorable ignorance among those who have gifts. It is not right for you to think that because you have a gift, you are to wave it before the people and try to get their minds upon that, because, if you do, you will be out of the will of God. Gifts and callings in the body of Christ may be irrevocable (Rom. 11:29), but remember that God calls you to account for properly administering the gift in a spiritual way after you have received it. It is not given to adorn you, but to sustain, build, edify, and bless the church. When God ministers through a member of the body of Christ and the church receives this edification, then all the members will rejoice together. God moves upon us as His offspring, as His choice, and as the fruit of the earth. He wants us to be elegantly clothed in wonderful raiment, even as our Master is.

His workings upon us may be painful, but the wise saint will remember that among those whom God chastens, it is the one who is trained by that chastening to whom *"it yields the peaceable fruit of righteousness"* (Heb. 12:11). Therefore, let Him do with you what seems good to Him, for He has His hand upon you; He will not willingly take it off until He has performed the thing He knows you need. So if He comes to sift you, be ready for the sifting. If He comes with chastisement, be ready for chastisement. If He comes with correction, be ready for correction. Whatever He wills, let Him do it, and He will bring you to the land of plenty. Oh, it is worth the world to be under the power of the Holy Spirit!

If He does not chasten you, if you sail placidly along without incident, without crosses, without persecutions, without trials, remember that *"if you are without chastening, of which all have become partakers, then you are illegitimate and not sons"* (Heb. 12:8). Therefore, *"examine yourselves as to whether you are in the faith"* (2 Cor. 13:5). Never forget that Jesus said this word: "They who hear My voice follow Me." (See John 10:27.) Jesus wants you all to follow; He wants you to have a clear ring to your testimony.

You are eternally saved by the power of God. Do not be led astray by anything; do not mistake your feelings for your salvation; do not take anybody's word for your salvation. Believe that God's Word is true. What does it say? *"He who believes in the Son has everlasting life; and he who does not believe the Son shall not see life, but the wrath of God abides on him"* (John 3:36).

When your will becomes entirely the will of God, then you are clearly in the place where the Holy Spirit can make Jesus Lord in your life, Lord over your purchases, Lord over your selling, Lord over your eating and your drinking, Lord over your clothing, and Lord over your choice of companions.

> *There are diversities of gifts, but the same Spirit. There are differences of ministries, but the same Lord. And there are diversities of activities, but it is the same God who works all in all. But the manifestation of the Spirit is given to each one for the profit of all.*
> (1 Cor. 12:4–7)

The variation of humanity is tremendous. Faces are different, so are physiques. Your whole body may be put together in such a way that one particular gift would not suit you at all, while it would suit another person.

So the Word of God deals here with varieties of gifts, meaning that these gifts perfectly meet the condition of each believer. That is God's plan. It may be that not one person would be led to claim all the gifts. Nevertheless, do not be afraid; the Scriptures are definite. Paul said that you do not need to come short in any gift (1 Cor. 1:7). God has wonderful things for you beyond what you have ever known. The Holy Spirit is so full of prophetic operations of divine power that it is marvelous what may happen after the Holy Spirit comes.

How He loosed me! I am no good without the Holy Spirit. The power of the Holy Spirit loosed my language. I was like my mother. She had no ability to speak. If she began to tell a story, she couldn't finish it. My father would say, "Mother, you will have to begin again." I was like that. I couldn't tell a story. I was bound. I had plenty of thoughts, but no language. But oh, after the Holy Spirit came!

When He came, I had a great desire for gifts. So the Lord caused me to see that it is possible for every believer to live in such holy anointing, such divine communion, such pressed-down measure (Luke 6:38) by the power of the Spirit, that every gift can be his.

But is there not a vast and appalling unconcern about possessing the gifts? You may ask a score of believers, chosen at random from almost any church, "Do you have any of the gifts of the Spirit?" The answer from all will be, "No," and it will be given in a tone and with a manner that conveys the thought that the believer is not surprised that he does not have the gifts, that he doesn't expect to have any of them, and that he does not expect to seek them. Isn't this terrible, when the living Word specifically exhorts us to *"earnestly desire the best gifts"* (1 Cor. 12:31)?

So in order that the gifts might be everything and in evidence, we have to see that we cease to live without His glory. He works with us, and we work with Him—cooperating, working together. This is divine. Surely this is God's plan.

God has brought you to the banquet, and He wants to send you away full. We are in a place where

God wants to give us visions. We are in a place where, in His great love, He is bending over us with kisses. Oh, how lovely is the kiss of Jesus, the expression of His love!

Oh, come, let us seek Him for the best gifts, and let us strive to be wise and to rightly divide the Word of Truth (2 Tim. 2:15), giving it forth in power so that the church may be edified and sinners may be saved.

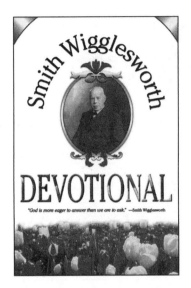

Smith Wigglesworth Devotional
Smith Wigglesworth

You are invited to journey with Smith Wigglesworth on a year-long trip that will quench your spiritual thirst while it radically transforms your faith. As you daily explore these challenging insights from the Apostle of Faith, you will connect with God's glorious power, cast out doubt, and see impossibilities turn into realities. Your prayer life will never be the same again when you personally experience the joy of seeing awesome, powerful results as you extend God's healing grace to others.

ISBN: 978-0-88368-574-7 • Trade • 560 pages

www.whitakerhouse.com